The Traveler's Complete Guide to Chiang Mai and Northern Thailand

John Hoskin

HKP

Text: John Hoskin

Illustrations: Santi Channonsruang and
Songsakdi Wongwang

Maps: Woranit Kayaras

Cover photograph by Dean Barrett

'Cover design by Yun Myung-Sook

Published by Hong Kong Publishing Company Ltd.,
and distributed in Thailand by Asia Book Company,
Ltd.

Designed by Alex Ma, 1A Communication Ltd.

Printed in Hong Kong by New Champion Printing
Co., Ltd.

ISBN: 962-7035-16-5   Reprinted 1986

CONTENTS

"An excellent and highly useful new guidebook"
Bangkok Post

"Designed for the spectrum of travellers from do-it-
yourselfers to tour-bus addicts, this attractive book
includes background history and key points of interest
in each section" *Asiaweek*

"If you do plan to visit this area, ignore Guide to
Chiang Mai and Northern Thailand at your peril"
Business Traveler

Acknowledgments

The author wishes to express his gratitude to the
Tourism Authority of Thailand for their kind and
generous assistance during the research of this book.
Individual thanks are due to Dhàrmnoon
Prachuabmoh, Deputy Governor of T.A.T.; Tassna
Wongrat, former Director of T.A.T. Chiang Mai;
Paisan Wangsai of T.A.T. Bangkok and researcher
Ratana Theprangsimankul. Above all, the author
acknowledges his debt to Woranit Kayaras of T.A.T.
who not only drove and guided him throughout the
North but also provided much invaluable information
while proving to be one of those rare beings, an
amiable traveling companion. Finally, many thanks to
Ruby who helped in so many ways.

Other books on Thailand published by Hong Kong
Publishing Company, Ltd. include:

**The Traveler's Complete Guide to
  Pattaya and Southeastern Thailand**
Images of Thailand
The Girls of Thailand
Traditional Thailand
Bangkok Only Yesterday
Noy of the Horny Toad and Other Anomalies
Memoirs of a Bangkok Warrior

INTRODUCTION

The Traveller's Complete Guide
To Chiang Mai & Northern Thailand

Northern Thailand is still largely a place unto itself. Admittedly it is not as isolated as it was just a few decades ago, and road, rail and air links are now well established. Nevertheless, the region manages to retain more than just an essence of its cultural and historical heritage, a heritage that is different from that of any other part of Thailand.

Quite simply the North is just that, different. The scenery, for a start, contrasts sharply with that of the adjoining Central Plains and is characterised by mountains, valleys, rivers, waterfalls and caves. Paddy fields and water buffalo give way to teak forests and work elephants; fruit and vegetables more common to temperate climes are cultivated in addition to rice and, this being the heart of the infamous 'Golden Triangle,' the opium poppy is illegally grown on many a hidden mountain slope.

Traditional art and architecture are again distinctive with the styles of the ancient Lannathai Kingdom, along with Burmese influences, characterising temples, sculpture and other art forms. Cottage industries producing numerous types of handicrafts for long special to the North are still flourishing while dances, cuisine, festivals and other cultural manifestations are distinct from those of other parts of the country.

The people, too, are different, with many northern Thais showing strains of Burmese and Lao traits and the

1

population of the region is made more varied by the presence of Thai Yais (Shans) from Burma and, most distinctive of all, by several different tribes of hillpeople who live virtually autonomous lives, mostly unaffected by mainstream society. Moreover, the male traveller will be delighted to learn that the girls of the North are generally thought to be the prettiest of all Thais.

Ultimately it is its history that indelibly marks the region as different. It was here that the great Lannathai Kingdom was established in the 13th century with Chiang Mai as its capital. But even before that small city kingdoms had left their mark. Despite mixed fortunes, including periods of Burmese domination, the North retained a sense of independence until the early 20th century.

Such separate development has instilled in the people a very real belief in their own identity and a pride in their traditional way of life. There is a retention of basic values and gentle manners and Northern Thais truly justify Thailand's old sobriquet of the 'Land of Smiles.'

Since the founding of the Lannathai Kingdom, Chiang Mai has remained the principal city of the North and, while preserving much of its cultural and historical fascination, it is today well geared to meet the needs of the traveller. However, there is far more to the region than just Chiang Mai and this book is a comprehensive attempt to provide factual information to enable the non-Thai speaker to explore the entire North. Together with cultural and historical background information, the book contains details on the facilities available and on what there is to do and see. Directions have been written in a manner to ensure that anyone can make it from place to place without getting lost.

The book is written with four kinds of travellers in mind: the principal type wants to see Chiang Mai; the second has hired a car either in Bangkok or Chiang Mai and intends making an extensive tour; the third is the determined do-it-yourselfer with time on his hands and a desire to travel by public transport, and the fourth type of traveller prefers to go by tour bus and for him the numerous daily tours arranged by Chiang Mai travel agencies have been listed.

The North

The North describes the area that makes up the dome of the elephant's head, referring to the oft-quoted similarity between Thailand's outline and that of the pachyderm's head and trunk. Its southern edge borders on an imaginary west-east line running through the towns of Tak and Phitsanulok. This is approximately the historic boundary between the former kingdoms of Lannathai and Ayutthaya although for the purposes of this book, the ancient town of Kamphaeng Phet, 67km southeast of Tak, has been included in the area.

The arterial road link is Highway 1 (part of the Asian Highway system) which runs from Bangkok to Chiang Rai, passing through Lampang from where Highway 11 branches off northwest to reach Chiang Mai, approximately 700km from the Thai capital. The northern railway line starting in Bangkok terminates in Chiang Mai from where there are good bus and air services to the main towns of the North.

Geographically, the region is intersected north-south by a number of rivers, principally the Ping, which flows through Chiang Mai, the Wang, the Yom and the Nan. In between the valleys is mostly hill country clothed in dense jungle and teak forests. Certain peaks are designated mountains although all are well below the tree line and Thailand's highest point, Doi Inthanon, reaches only 2,565 m.

Because of the elevation, the North generally has a more temperate climate than that of Bangkok but summer afternoons can be hotter, especially in the valleys and the eastern part of the region. The best time to visit is during the cool season from late October to the end of February when the average temperature is 21°C and much cooler at night. The coolest months are December and January when the mornings are crisp, the days warm and sunny and the evenings chilly. This season coincides with the beautiful Loy Krathong festival (end-Oct or early-Nov) and Chiang Mai's Flower Carnival (Feb) — flowers bloom and many temperate fruit such as strawberries are in season during January/February, and the opium poppy also flowers at this time.

The hot season, which can be dusty and uncomfortable, is from early March to the end of May when the average temperature is 29.9°C. The hottest month is April. The rainy season runs from early June to the end of October with an average temperature of 25.5°C and September being the wettest month. The rains are not continuous and are generally confined to short, sharp bursts. However, many of the unsurfaced roads become impassable at this time.

With regard to major sights, spectacular scenery, hilltribe villages, temples and ancient ruins are fairly evenly spread throughout the North. Only the important remains of the Sukhothai Kingdom — at Sukhothai, Si Satchanalai and Kamphaeng Phet — are clustered in the southern part of the region.

Getting Started

Below are some of the things you need to know before setting off. Other background information on, for example, hilltribes, is given in the appendices.

Visas. There are several kinds of visas for travel to Thailand. A tourist visa allows a 60-day stay. Two or four photographs depending on the embassy, and 300 baht are required. It can be extended if the visitor can provide a good reason, e.g. sickness, but the extension must be requested 2-3 days before the original visa's expiry date.

A transit visa is good for 30 days. It also costs 300 baht and the visitor must possess a valid onward air ticket. Rules for extending are the same as for a tourist visa.

The tourist arriving at the airport without a visa is allowed to stay for 15 days; these visas cannot be extended.

Visas can be extended at the Immigration Division on Soi Suam Plu off Sathorn Road in Bangkok or at the Immigration Office at 30 Moo 3 Tambon Chang Puak, Chotana Road, Chiang Mai.

Foreign Exchange. Most banks in the North will exchange major foreign currencies for Thai baht at the official government rate. The rate changes slightly from day to day but is usually in the area of 26 baht for one U.S. dollar. Exact rates for each currency are printed daily in the English-language newspapers. Hotels and other establishments generally give much lower rates. If travelling in remote areas be sure to carry small bills; few shops have change for a 500-baht note.

For up-to-date information. The Tourism Authority of Thailand (TAT) can help plan an itinerary tailored to a tourist's interests or render assistance with special problems. The Bangkok office is on Rajdamnern Nok Avenue near the Rajdamnern Boxing Stadium. The Chiang Mai office is at 135 Praisanee Road on the corner of Ta Pae Road near Nawarat Bridge.

Bus services. There are eight scheduled services daily by public bus to Chiang Mai, departing from Bangkok's Northern bus station Ta-lard-mor-chid on Phaholyothin Road. Tel: 279-4484. Fares are 240 baht one way and 460 baht return. The journey takes about nine hours.

Private bus companies offer a similar service by luxury air-conditioned tour coaches with fares comparable to those above. Major companies include (first address is Bangkok, second is Chiang Mai office):

Bancha Tour & Trading,
Petchburi Road opposite Metro Cinema. Tel: 251-5087, 251-9022
Saeng Tawan Cinema, 5/4 Chang Klan at Sri Dornchai. Tel: 234688

Cosmos,
52/8 Thai Style Bldg., Suriwongse Road.
Tel: 233-5396, 233-7593
Porn Ping Hotel, 46-48 Charoenprathet Road.
Tel: 235405

Setthee (Grand),
590-592 Ploenchit Road. Tel: 252-0335, 252-0337
In front of Chiang Inn Hotel, 100 Chang Klan Road.
Tel: 234723, 236558

Indra,
next to Indra Regent Hotel, Rajprarob Road.
Tel: 251-6197, 252-3402
next to Suriwongse Hotel, 110 Chang Klan Road.
Tel: 234638

Pimarn,
78-82 Rajaprasong. Tel: 251-6428, 251-0631
147/6 Chang Klan Road. Tel: 234742

Poy Luang,
137/3 Gaysorn Road. Tel: 252-0200, 252-0221
80/1 Sridonchai Road. Tel: 235943

Sri Thong,
Metro Shopping Centre. Tel: 251-9296, 511-0232
opposite Diamond Hotel, Charoenprathet Road.
Tel: 236179

Thavorn Farm,
Northern Bus Terminal. Tel: 279-5044, 279-5850
next to Saeng Tawan Cinema. Tel: 235350

From Chiang Mai there are numerous public bus
services daily to the major towns of the North. The
principal bus stations are Chang Puak (White
Elephant) on Chotana Road from where buses serve
destinations within Chiang Mai Province, and Chiang
Mai Arcade on the Superhighway where buses leave
for towns outside Chiang Mai Province. Also, some
buses for Chiang Rai and Lampang, as well as
Lamphun, leave from the station on the Old Chiang
Mai Road (H 106) on the east bank of the Ping river
opposite Nawarat Bridge.

Trains services. The State Railways of Thailand
operates two daily departures to/from Chiang Mai,
departing Bangkok from Hua Lumpong Station.
Tel: 223-7020.

Rapid Train leaves Bangkok at 3.45 p.m., arriving
Chiang Mai at 6.20 a.m.
Express Train leaves Bangkok at 6.00 p.m., arriving
Chiang Mai at 7.50 a.m.
Chiang Mai Railway Station. Tel: 236094
Rapid Train leaves Chiang Mai at 2.45 p.m.,
arriving Bangkok at 5.40 a.m.
Express Train leaves Chiang Mai at 4.50 p.m.,
arriving Bangkok at 6.30 a.m.

One-way fares range from 232 baht for a seat to 673
baht for an air-conditioned sleeping berth (sleeping
berths available only on Express Train). Advance
booking (up to 10 days) is recommended. The

Northern Railway line terminates in Chiang Mai and although it serves some stations south of that city — e.g. Phitsanulok, Uttaradit, Lampang and Lamphun — arrival/departure times do not make the train a convenient means of transportation around the North.

Airlines. Thai Airways operates five Boeing 737 return flights daily Bangkok-Chiang Mai; all are direct (flying time one hour) except for one flight which stops at Phitsanulok. One-way fare is 1,100 baht; return 2,200 baht.

From Chiang Mai, the domestic airline flies daily services to Chiang Rai, Mae Hong Son, Phitsanulok and Phrae; four times weekly to Nan and three times weekly to Lampang. All these flights are by Shorts 330 turboprops.

For flight reservations telephone Bangkok 281-1633 or Chiang Mai 233559, 233560, 234150, 235462. Advance booking is recommended especially in the winter high season.

Car rentals. Cars can be rented at several agencies both in Bangkok and in Chiang Mai. The most popular are Hertz (on Ploenchit Road, Bangkok. Tel: 252-4918. Or Chiang Mai Inter-Service Co. Ltd., 442 Charoen Muang Road, Chiang Mai. Tel: 235925) and Avis (at Rama Tower Hotel, 981 Silom Road, Bangkok. Tel: 234-1010 Ext. 257. Or 14/14 Huay Kaew Road, Chiang Mai. Tel: 221813).

For a Toyota Crown Deluxe, Hertz charges 1,800 baht daily self drive or 2,000 baht with driver, plus 4 baht per kilometre and 300 baht per day for driver if included. For the same, Avis charges 1,080 baht per day self drive or 2,200 with driver. Same per km. surcharge as Hertz.

In Chiang Mai most of the top hotels can also arrange car rentals while Chong Charoen Co. Ltd., 52/2 Sri Dorn Chai Road, A, Muang (tel: 236588, 234901, 232452) hires out chauffeur-driven cars, minibuses and landrovers.

Motorcycle rentals. Motorcycles can be rented in Chiang Mai from some guesthouses and from a number of shops on Moon Muang Road (near Daret's Restaurant), in front of Porn Ping Road on Charoenprathet Road and in front of Pornsawas Tour opposite the Night Bazaar on Chang Klan Road. Charges (excluding gas) are around 100 baht per day (8.00 a.m. to 5.00 p.m.) for an 80cc machine, 120 baht for 100cc and 150 baht for 125cc. Be warned: the motorbike is the hirer's responsibility and machine should be carefully checked before use — spare parts are imported and therefore expensive. Passport is usually taken as security.

Bicycle rentals. Bicycles can be rented in Chiang Mai at some guesthouses and at shops on Moon Muang Road near Daret's Restaurant. Rates are between 25-30 baht per day. Passport held as security.

Tour agencies. There are a number of tour and travel agencies in Chiang Mai offering half- and full-day sightseeing trips in and around the city. Most major hotels have tour counters but the two main operators are 'Chiangmai Travel Centre' with offices at Rincome Hotel on Huay Kaew Road (tel: 221692) and 'World Travel Service' with counters at the following hotels: Chiang Inn, Chiang Mai Hills, Orchid, Rincome and Chiang Mai Palace.

Trekking agencies. There are also a number of agencies specialising in trekking tours in the Chiang Mai area. Duration is generally from 3 to 7 days with overnight stops made in hilltribe villages. Prices start from around 500 baht for a 3-day trek (including food).

Three of the main trekking agencies are: Summit Tribal Trek, Thai Charoen Hotel, Ta Pae Road (tel: 236640); Orbit Tribal Trekking, 2 Rajamanka Soi 2 (near Thai-German Dairy) and Manit Tribal Travel Agency, 82 Chaiyaphum Road (tel: 234860).

WARNING: Some trekking tours have been known to lead travellers into sensitive areas with unfortunate consequences — robbery if not worse. Recently, police have been trying to exercise greater control on trekking tours, asking for registration of routes, trek members etc. It is, therefore, advisable to check with the authorities (e.g. TAT) in advance that a proposed trek is safe. Moreover, it is completely foolish to trek without an experienced guide — hostile elements can be found in some areas and being an ignorant tourist is no safeguard.

Driving in the North. A valid international driver's

licence is required for driving a car or motorcycle in Thailand. Outside the cities the top speed allowed is 100 kph. Vehicles are meant to drive on the left-hand side of the road; this fact is noted here since it cannot always be determined by first-hand observation.

Outside the towns, traffic on the highways is generally light although a wide berth should be given to 10-wheel trucks and long-distance buses — most drivers are speed freaks, some in both senses of the term.

The fact that traffic is mostly light does unfortunately mean that people in the country districts have a poorly developed road sense. Vehicles, especially motorbikes and bicycles, are apt to shoot out of side roads without a glance for on-coming traffic, or else suddenly make a right turn without prior warning. Expect the unexpected is a good rule. Pedestrians, water buffalo, pigs, dogs, chickens etc, although unpredictable and often showing suicidal tendencies, are not fair game. Gentle warning in advance by the car horn is advised when overtaking anything but an immobile object.

Road signs, both directions and warnings of hazards, are in most cases good. Major place names are written in both Thai and English while international hazard signs are followed.

Electrical current. Electricity is 220 volts and 50 cycles and can be found in most urban areas of Thailand.

Medical. Most of the major communicable diseases have been eradicated but to be on the safe side, drink only boiled or bottled water. Crushed ice served at roadside stalls should also be avoided. If travelling in the countryside or jungle areas, anti-malaria tablets should be taken as a precaution; there are several brands available on the market. Almost every large town has a hospital with a staff fully capable of handling most emergencies. The principal hospital in Chiang Mai catering to foreigners is the McCormick, 135 Kaew Nawarat Road (tel: 236010, 236107).

Notes on using this book

This book assumes Chiang Mai as being the base for

all excursions throughout the North and itineraries are described as starting and finishing in that city. It is, of course, possible for the traveller to work out his own itinerary, touring without taking Chiang Mai as his base, and for this purpose all major roads and their intersections are indicated in the text.

In compiling this book the author used three sets of maps as well as having the assistance of an experienced driver/guide. The maps in this book, therefore, have been drawn after extensive travel throughout the North and to the best of the author's knowledge contain correct information.

To supplement the maps, the text provides detailed descriptions of turns to be taken and distances to be travelled. If the text notes a 'KM 109', the reference is to the kilometre post sitting at the side of the road. If the notation says only '5.6km', it is the distance computed by the car's odometer. (To convert kilometres to miles multiply by 0.6214.)

All highways in Thailand are numbered and in the text are indicated by, for example, 'Highway 1' or simply 'H 1.' Unless otherwise stated, roads are surfaced. Roads indicated as being 'dirt,' 'laterite,' 'track,' etc. are often impassable by ordinary car in the rainy season (early June to end of October) and local advice should be sought before travelling such routes during this period.

The spelling of place names in this book is that which is most commonly used, but the traveller should be aware that there is more than one system of romanized Thai and differences in spelling will be found, especially in street names.

The following Thai words may prove useful in deciphering maps and place names:

Amphoe: secondary administrative centre
Ban: village
Changwat: primary administrative centre
Doi: mountain
Huai: stream
Khao: hill
Klong: canal
Mae Nam: river
Mon: hill (northern dialect)

Soi: lane

Tham: cave

Thanon: road

The following Thai words refer to aspects of temple buildings:

Bot: the main shrine of a temple where monks are ordained.

Chedi: now synonymous with **stupa** and is a solid monument, usually with a pointed spire, built to enshrine relics of the Buddha or those of his disciples, or to contain the ashes of the dead.

Mondop: square building housing a Buddha image or other sacred object.

Naga: mythical king of snakes; most commonly sculpted as a balustrade to stairs leading up to a temple.

Prang: a structure in imitation of a Khmer tower with a finger-like spire.

Thammas: pulpit or preaching chair.

Viharn: main hall of a temple used for day to day services.

Wat: temple; refers to the whole compound.

CHIANG MAI

Chiang Mai, Thailand's second largest city, is pleasantly located on the banks of the Ping river and set amid a lush, fertile plain at an average elevation of 300 m above sea level. The plain is partially surrounded by forested mountains and to the west the area is dominated by the majestic eminence of Doi Suthep which rises to over 1,000 m.

It is an old city with a history stretching back 700 years and until the early 20th century it was virtually politically independent and more or less geographically isolated. Today, Chiang Mai is readily accessible from Bangkok although it was only in the 1920s that the northern railway line was completed, thus opening up the region. Prior to that a journey north took several weeks of arduous travel by river and elephant back.

Such separate development has allowed the city to preserve its unique character which has given rise to such sobriquets as 'Flower of the North' and to the idea of a Shangri-La typified by beautiful scenery, ancient temples, traditional handicrafts and customs and a people unaffected by the modern pace of life.

This glowing reputation is not without justification and Chiang Mai is a storehouse of cultural manifestations evolving from a long and rich past. However, while its heritage has not been squandered, it would be totally misleading to suggest that the city has not changed over the years. The attractions remain in profusion but Chiang Mai is no longer the quiet town of charming wooden houses that it was just a few decades ago.

The traveller who thinks only of the 'Flower of the North' and forgets that the city is also Thailand's second largest will be disappointed. True, Chiang Mai is only one fortieth the size of metropolitan Bangkok, but it is expanding rapidly in all directions and the confines of the old city wall and moat have long since been overcome. Traffic congestion is mounting,

MAP OF THE NORTH

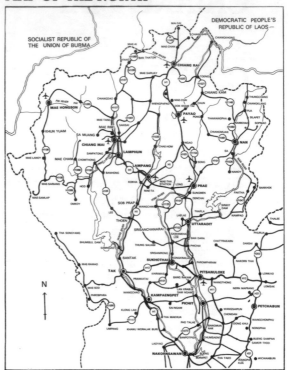

industrialization lies just around the corner and far from slumbering in the past, the place is a busy, vibrant commercial and administrative centre. It is by no means as hectic nor as built-up as Bangkok — that would be a most unfair comparison — yet at the same time it has not been overlooked by the 20th century.

Progress is inevitable and Chiang Mai has undoubtedly lost much of its traditional charm. Nevertheless, modern concrete buildings have not totally obliterated ancient temples, craftsmen still ply their several time-honoured trades and the people continue to take pride in their heritage and place more emphasis on **sanuk** (having fun) than on questing after material success. Changes there have been, but 700 years of history does not vanish overnight and the traveller should be prepared to appreciate what survives and not regret what has been lost.

Of course, modernization has its positive side. Chiang Mai now has a well developed tourist infrastructure with a host of hotels in all price ranges from deluxe to guesthouse. Restaurants, too, abound and in addition to those specialising in northern Thai food, there are others which collectively offer just about the whole gamut of international cuisines. Nightlife attractions and shopping facilities are also well developed as are sightseeing arrangements and communication links to other towns of the North.

What's where

The original city of Chiang Mai was constructed several hundred metres back from the west bank of the Ping river and was surrounded by a fortified wall and moat. Today, only the latter remains and the walls have long since vanished although the five principal city gates have been restored to their original appearance. These are: White Elephant Gate **(Chang Puak)** in the north; Ta Pae Gate in the east; Chiang Mai and Suan Prang Gates both in the south and, to the west, Suan Dork Gate.

CITY MAP OF CHIANG MAI

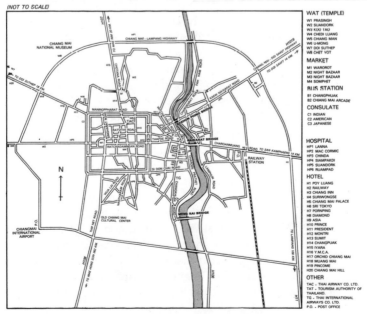

15

*Old City Gate
in Chiang Mai*

For some years now the city has been expanding beyond the old moat with the earliest of the new developments taking place between the eastern wall and the Ping river. This area, traversed west-east by the main thoroughfare of Ta Pae Road, running from Ta Pae Gate to Nawarat Bridge, today comprises downtown Chiang Mai. Here are to be found the principal shopping and business centres along with several of the major hotels, including three of the top six (Chiang Mai Palace, Suriwongse and Chiang Inn).

On the eastern bank of the river are the railway station, the nearby main post office and the fourth of the city's leading hotels, the Poy Luang next to the Superhighway. Spanning the Ping river are four bridges, namely, from north to south, Ping River Bridge (crossed by the Superhighway), Nakhonping Bridge, Nawarat Bridge and Mengrai Bridge.

The most recent areas of expansion are to the southwest, where the airport is sited, and to the west where there is Chiang Mai University and, along the way, the two other top hotels (arguably the city's finest), the Orchid and the Rincome.

Getting around

Chiang Mai has a public bus service, the so-called 'yellow buses,' but this has been dubbed the world's slowest mass transport system and the circuitous routes are really only useful as cheap ways of taking a town tour for those with plenty of time on their hands.

The easiest way of getting about is by minibus **(song thaew)** — pick-up trucks with benches and a roof. These ply more or less regular routes although not direct as passengers are picked up and dropped according to demand. The standard fare for going anywhere in town is 4 baht.

A slower, more leisurely means of transport is the trishaw or pedal **samlor** which seats two at a squeeze. A short trip should cost around 5 baht.
Chiang Mai has hardly any cruising taxis such as are found in abundance in Bangkok, although usually unmarked taxis congregate outside the major hotels. A journey within the city should not cost more than 30 baht.

NB: Fares for all means of transportation other than public buses should be agreed with the driver **before** embarking on a journey.

History

Chiang Mai was founded in 1296 by King Mengrai as the capital of his rapidly expanding Lannathai Kingdom and from that time it has remained the principal city of the North, surviving ups and downs that included Burmese occupation and one period of abandonment.

Mengrai was a Thai-Lao prince, the son of King Lao Meng who had established a small kingdom centred on Chiang Saen in the far north. This area had formerly been under the control of the powerful Khmers but with increasing waves of immigrants from southern China, the Thai people were gradually coming to unite and gaining strength.

On succeeding his father, Mengrai gathered several small tribes together and quickly set about enlarging his domain, moving south from Chiang Saen, first to Chiang Rai which he founded as his capital in 1262.

Then, after defeating the old Mon Kingdom of Haripunchai (Lamphun today), he chose for strategic reasons what is now Chiang Mai as the power centre of his newly conquered lands which he named Anachak Lannathai.

According to legend, Mengrai decided on the site for his new capital because of three lucky omens that were supposedly seen there — namely two white sambar deer, two white barking deer and a white mouse with a family of five. On a more practical level, Mengrai consulted his allies, King Ramkamhaeng of Sukhothai and King Ngam Muang of Phayao, and together they worked out the dimensions and fortifications of the city which was named Nopphaburi Si Nakhonphing Chiang Mai, meaning 'New City' (the first part of the name being the Sanskrit translation of Chiang Mai).

It is believed that some 90,000 workers were involved in the construction of the city which was originally centered on Wat Chiang Man. However, Mengrai's successors several times altered the layout and relocated the fortifications, and the present siting of the walls and moat dates from the early 19th century.

King Mengrai died in 1317, reputedly struck by lightning, but not before he had consolidated his kingdom and established a ruling dynasty. Chiang Mai prospered, cordial relations continued with Sukhothai while 10 years after the death of King Ngam Muang in 1328, Phayao was annexed to the Lannathai Kingdom. At the height of its power Chiang Mai was the effective capital of most of the region north of Sukhothai and the Lannathai Kingdom covered the present day provinces of Chiang Mai, Lamphun, Lampang, Mae Hong Son, Chiang Rai, Phrae, Nan and Phayao.

Security existed so long as Sukhothai held sway in the south but the later Thai kingdom of Ayutthaya, centred on the Chao Phya basin, had become powerful by the 14th century and was to upset the status quo. King Boromaraja I of Ayutthaya led repeated campaigns against Sukhothai with the latter finally capitulating at Kamphaeng Phet in 1378. The fall of the first Thai kingdom would undoubtedly have come earlier had not Boromaraja's initial forays been frustrated by the presence of Lannathai troops who had come south to assist their ally.

Chiang Mai's support of Sukhothai had incensed Ayutthaya and Boromaraja quickly set high sights on Lannathai but two campaigns failed to take it, the last one coming to an end on Boromaraja's death in 1388. There then followed a period of uneasy relations and occasional warfare between Ayutthaya and Lannathai.

The golden age of Chiang Mai and the Lannathai Kingdom blossomed in the mid-15th century during the reign of King Tilokaraja who ruled from 1442 to 1487. He led an offensive against Ayutthaya, taking briefly the town of Kamphaeng Phet, but as well as being a formidable warrior he was also a stalwart upholder of the Buddhist faith, responsible for the building of a number of temples and for arranging the 8th World Buddhist Council to be held in Chiang Mai in 1477.

Sporadic warfare between Chiang Mai and Ayutthaya continued in the 16th century with the former suffering a severe defeat at Lampang in 1515. By now the Mengrai dynasty was weakening and losing its power and a new enemy, Burma, was presenting an ever-increasing threat in the west. After controversies over succession and other internal drains on power,

Wat Phra Singh

Chiang Mai finally fell and Lannathai became a vassal state of Burma in 1556. For the next two centuries the North was to be under the sovereignty of Burma with Chiang Mai being ruled by either puppet kings or by Burmese overlords. During these 200 years Burmese dominance faltered only occasionally with Lannathai briefly becoming a vassal of Ayutthaya and, once, enjoying a spell of independence.

Holding the North, the Burmese turned their attention to Ayutthaya and it was not until after they had attacked and sacked that city that the Thais, reunited under King Taksin, who had quickly set up a new Thai capital at Thonburi, finally expelled the invaders. Gradually moving north, Taksin managed to re-take Chiang Mai in 1775 but, after an unsuccessful attempt by the Burmese to win it back in the following year, it was decided to abandon the city since its population had been greatly reduced and impoverished by almost continual warfare. Accordingly, Taksin moved the surviving inhabitants to Lampang and Chiang Mai was to remain deserted for the next 20 years.

Then, in 1796, King Rama I, Taksin's successor and the founder of Bangkok as Thailand's capital, appointed Phraya Kawila, son of the Prince of Lampang, as the Governor-Prince of a revived Chiang Mai and he was to establish a line of hereditary rulers of the city. At first Chiang Mai remained semi-autonomous as the capital of the 'Northern Circle' but with moves towards greater centralization taken in the late 19th century, the power of the princes was gradually eroded. However, it was not until 1938 that the office of the Governor-Prince was formally abolished. By then Chiang Mai was officially just another provincial capital under the control of the Ministry of the Interior of the central government in Bangkok.

Temples

Nowhere is Chiang Mai's glorious past more evident than in the city's many temples. Most are in the traditional northern style with two- or three-tiered roofs with low eaves and finely carved pediments, but there are also Burmese influences and sufficient architectural variety — notably in the design of **chedis** — as to make a comprehensive tour rewarding.

For the traveller with little time to spare, the five most important or most interesting temples are **Wat Phra Singh, Wat Chedi Luang, Wat Chiang Man, Wat Chet Yot** and **Wat Suan Dork.** The other temples described here are also well-worth visiting and should be included along with the top five if one is to gain a true insight into Chiang Mai's past. For the sake of convenience they are divided into those which are located in the city centre and those which lie a little way outside.

Within the city

Wat Phra Singh, on the corner of Singharat and Rajadamnoen Roads, was constructed in 1345 by King Pha Yu of the Mengrai dynasty who built the large

Wat Mengrai

21

chedi to hold the ashes of his father, King Kam Fu. The comparatively modern **viharn** is the first building encountered beyond the entrance, but to the right of this is a more interesting 14th century scripture repository. Typical of its kind, this small building is characterised by a two-tier, three-level roof and richly carved wooden sides decorated with inlaid coloured glass, all of which is raised on a high stucco-covered stone base.

Behind the **viharn** is the **bot** with fine woodcarving and stucco work decoration, but the most important building in the compound is the small old chapel on the left known as **Phra Viharn Lai Kam.** This attractive structure, with typical northern style stucco work over the doorway, houses the important gilded bronze statue of **Phra Singh Buddha.** A good deal of legend surrounds the possible origins of this image with local belief holding that it is some 1,500 years old and was originally brought to Thailand from Sri Lanka. This, however, would seem unlikely since the statue is in the early Chiang Saen style and whatever its ancient history, it is known to have been brought to Chiang Mai from Chiang Rai in 1400 by King Saen Muang Ma. The original head was stolen in 1922 and the present one is a replica.

The walls of the chapel are decorated with northern Thai narrative mural paintings with the one on the right taking its theme from the story of **Phra San Tong,** and the one on the left depicting the legend of **Suwannahong.** These are especially interesting for their portrayal of northern dress, customs and scenes from daily life.

Wat Chedi Luang, on Phra Pokklao Road, is famous for its massive, though partially ruined **chedi.** First built in 1401 by King Saen Muang Ma, the **chedi** was enlarged to a height of 86m by King Tilokaraja in 1454 but it was damaged by an earthquake in 1545 and never restored. Nevertheless, what remains is still most impressive and on one side there is a niche containing a sitting Buddha.

The **viharn** is also worthy of note being a good example of local monastic architecture, and the **nagas** flanking the entrance steps are considered to be the finest of their kind in the North. Inside the **viharn** is a large standing Buddha.

To the left of the entrance to the compound is a tall gum tree inhabited by a swarm of bees and nearby is Chiang Mai's 'city pillar' **(Sao Inthakin)**, representing the spirit of the city and guarded over by a statue of the giant **Tao Kumpakan.**

Wat Phan Tao lies directly behind Wat Chedi Luang. It is not one of the city's most important temples. The temple consists of a wooden **bot** and **viharn** in a good state of repair.

Wat Duang Di, a little to the north just behind the law courts on Ratvithi Road, has exceptionally fine carved wooden pediments.

Wat Mengrai lies a little to the southwest of Wat Chedi Luang on Rajmankha Road Lane 6. The temple buildings are not of special interest but what is remarkable is the superbly carved and highly ornate stucco entrance way facing the street.

Wat Chiang Man, on Rajaphakinar Road in the north-eastern corner of the old city, is probably Chiang Mai's oldest temple built by King Mengrai who is supposed to have resided at this site while his city was being constructed.

Inside the entrance are two **viharns**; both have richly carved wooden pediments but the building on the right is the more interesting since it enshrines two of Chiang Mai's most famous Buddha images. The building is usually kept locked but is open to the public on Sundays and Buddhist holidays from 9 a.m. to 5 p.m. One of the images is the tiny crystal figurine of **Phra Setang Khamani** set on a gold base and topped with a gold headdress. It is believed to have been first presented to Queen Chama Devi of Haripunchai in the 7th century and later brought to Chiang Mai after King Mengrai's victory over Haripunchai. The workmanship is not of the first order although the image is greatly revered as having the power to bring rain and is featured in a procession around town during the Songkran festival in April.

The other image is a stone Buddha, known as **Phra Sila**, carved in bas-relief and displaying fine craftsmanship. The style is unusual to Thailand and it is generally supposed that the statue was produced in India more than a thousand years ago.

Behind the **viharn** is a square **chedi** in typical Lannathai style except for the elephant buttresses decorating the base which are a Sri Lankan influence. To the left is the **bot** in front of which is a stone inscription dated 1581 and stating King Mengrai as the founder of the temple along with dates of early restoration work.

Wat Cha Si Phum, on Wichayanon Road outside the north-east corner of the old moat near the President Hotel, has a fine wooden scripture repository as well as a **viharn** with a nicely carved pediment, a **bot** and an excellent **chedi.**

Continuing around the corner of the moat there are two temples on Manee Noparat Road. The first, **Wat Pa Pao**, is fascinating for its Burmese-Shan architectural style while, a little farther along, **Wat Chiang Yuen** is notable for its large brick **chedi** covered with stucco and coloured ceramics.

In Ta Pae Road, going towards Ta Pae Gate, are four temples: **Wat Saen Fang** and **Wat Chettawan** on the right, and **Wat Bupparam** and **Wat Mahawan** on the left.

Wat Saen Fang is in Burmese style and its charm is enhanced by its approach of a narrow naga-flanked lane leading directly off the busy street into a tiny patch of serenity.

Wat Chet Yot

More or less opposite is Wat Bupparam which has a well decorated **viharn**, while a few metres farther up the road on the same side, Wat Mahawan has a large Burmese-style **chedi** and some good woodcarving on the main temple buildings. On the opposite side of the road is Wat Chettawan distinguished by three **chedis** and excellent examples of the woodcarver's art on the portico of the **viharn.**

Wat Chang Khong, on Loi Kroa Road near the Suriwongse Hotel, is remarkable for its splendid tiered roof.

Outside city centre

There are four principal temples lying outside the city centre proper which can be covered in a rough loop beginning at Suan Dork Gate.

Wat Suan Dork lies off to the left of Cherng Doi (Suthep) Road 1.1km west of Suan Dork Gate. The

Wat Koo Tao

'Flower Garden Temple' occupies a peaceful compound on the site of the former pleasure gardens of the early Lannathai kings which, in the late 14th century, were set aside as a sanctuary for the famous monk Phra Maha Sumana Thera. According to legend, Sumana Thera, following a dream, had discovered some holy relics buried in the ground and part of these were to be enshrined in the **chedi** built at Wat Suan Dork in 1383. (The remaining relics were kept at Wat Phrathat on Doi Suthep.)

The temple buildings seen today have been completely restored and there is little that is of architectural interest. The main hall is, however, the largest in the North and contains a sitting Buddha plus a number of smaller images.

The **bot**, a few metres beyond the hall, houses the Chiang Saen-style image of **Phra Chao Kao Tu**, a beautiful bronze sitting Buddha that was made in 1504 during the reign of King Muang Kaew.

Next to the temple is the cemetery for Chiang Mai's nobility with white stones marking the last resting place of the city's rulers, princes and other royalty.

Wat Suan Dork owes its impressiveness to its size and location rather than to any architectural beauty, yet it is an important temple and is the centre of a major religious ceremony during the Songkran festival which attracts a great number of devotees.

Festival at Chiang Mai University Campus

Wat Umong lies at the end of a side road off to the left of Cherng Doi Road 1.2km beyond the turning for Wat Suan Dork. Here, amid a tranquil grove where each tree bears a plaque containing a wise saying in Thai, Chinese and English, are the remains of a monastery founded by King Mengrai in 1296.

Little survives of the original structure other than a ruined **chedi** mounted on an extensive brick base beneath which are underground chambers where hermits once meditated. In the crypt are niches, some still containing Buddha images.

The ruins are approached by a flight of steps at the base of which is a statue of a **yak** guardian and at the top is a replica of Emperor Ashoka's famous pillar in India.

Although little remains of Wat Umong, the ruins do hold a certain fascination largely due to the serenity of the location.

Behind the temple is a small but attractive open zoo containing deer, wild buffalo and bears. There is also a pool and pathways affording pleasant walks through the woods.

Wat Chet Yot is on the left of the Superhighway about 1km beyond the junction with Huai Kaeo Road by the Rincome Hotel. The temple, correctly called **Wat Photharam Maha Viharn**, ranks among Chiang Mai's most important for both its historical and architectural interest.

Generally accepted to have been built by King Tilokaraja in 1455, it derives its popular name from the seven **(chet)** spires of its square **chedi**, the unusual design of which was copied from a temple in Pagan, Burma, itself a copy of the Mahabodhi temple in Bodh Gaya, India, where the Buddha achieved Enlightenment. The sides of the **chedi** (partially destroyed during a Burmese invasion) are beautifully decorated with celestial figures in stucco relief, and in the central spire there is a niche containing a Buddha image.

Next to the main structure are two other **chedis**, the larger one containing the ashes of King Tilokaraja. The two bo trees in the rear are said to have been grown from seeds of the tree under which the Buddha achieved Enlightenment.

Apart from its architectural interest, Wat Chet Yot is historically important as it was here that the 8th World Buddhist Council was convened in 1477 during which revisions of the **Tripitaka** (Buddhist teachings) were made.

Wat Koo Tao can be reached from Wat Chet Yot by continuing east along the Superhighway for 800 m, turning right at the traffic lights down Chotana Road and then, after 1km, left down the narrow Chang Puak Road Lane 6.

There is little of interest about the Burmese-style temple itself but its **chedi** is most unusual if not unique. Reputedly built in 1613 to contain the ashes of a Burmese ruler of Chiang Mai, it is in the form of what looks like five melon shapes (sometimes likened to alms bowls) superimposed on one another in descending order of size. In each orb are four niches containing Buddha statues.

Wat Sao Hin, off to the right of the airport highway (H 1141) just beyond KM 4, is rarely visited although it possesses a small but exquisite **viharn**, a tiny **bot** with a finely carved portico and a white Burmese-style **chedi**. It is about 500 years old and although somewhat off the beaten track is well worth visiting.

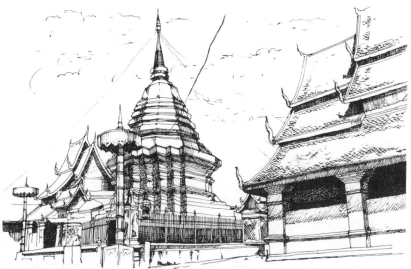

Wat Phrathat, Doi Suthep

Other Places Of Interest

Chiang Mai National Museum, located on the Superhighway close to Wat Chet Yot, is small but well maintained. On the ground floor are Buddha heads, images and other artifacts from Chiang Saen, Haripunchai, Sukhothai, Lop Buri and Ayutthaya periods. Especially noteworthy is a large bronze Buddha head in early Chiang Saen style. The back and top are incomplete but the face is quite remarkable. On the first floor are a collection of howdahs, coffin covers, plus displays of hilltribe costumes and northern-style household utensils. In the grounds outside are two ancient kilns.

The museum is open from 9 a.m. to noon and 1 p.m. to 4.30 p.m. Wednesday to Sunday. Entrance is free except for 2 baht on Saturday and Sunday.

Chiang Mai Zoological Park is the largest zoo in Thailand containing over 500 animals housed in pens set in the open amid extensive, attractively landscaped grounds — but note the site occupies a hillside and there are plenty of ups and downs.

Meo Hilltribe Women

The zoo, located just over 5km from the city off to the left of Huai Kaeo Road just before it begins to rise up towards Doi Suthep, is open daily from 8 a.m. to 5 p.m. Admission: adults 5 baht, children (under 135 cm!) 2 baht, cars 10 baht.

Just before the entrance to the zoo on the same side of the road is **Huay Kaeo Arboretum** (open 8 a.m. to 5 p.m.) which offers pleasant walks among trees and flowers.

Chiang Mai University & Tribal Research Centre. A few hundred metres before the zoo is Chiang Mai University which occupies a large and beautiful campus. Of special interest here is the Tribal Research Centre (open 8.30 a.m. to 4.30 p.m. Monday to Friday) which houses a small but fascinating museum of hilltribe artifacts which provide an excellent introduction to the culture of the various hilltribes of northern Thailand.

Ladda Land is a recreational park 2km along Kankhlong Chonpratan Mae Taeng Road which leads off right from Huai Kaeo Road near Chiang Mai Hills hotel. (Open daily from 8 a.m. to 5 p.m. Admission: adults 5 baht, children 3 baht.) Attractions include performances of Northern dances daily at 11 a.m. (also at 2 p.m. on Saturday and Sunday), landscaped gardens, orchids, museum, handicrafts shop, small restaurant, children's playground and typical Northern Thai houses. Also horse and carriage rides around the grounds (10 baht). A popular place with Chiang Mai residents and good for the children.

Outside Chiang Mai

There are a number of interesting half- and full-day trips than can be made from Chiang Mai. Major travel agencies offer a comprehensive programme of sightseeing tours or, alternatively, most places can be reached by public bus or minibus.

Doi Suthep, Phuping Palace & Meo Village

The most popular short excursion from Chiang Mai is to Doi Suthep, the mountain that majestically overlooks the city 16km away to the west. The journey follows H 1004 (Huai Kaeo Road from the city) and minibuses from Doi Suthep leave from White Elephant Gate (the fare up is 30 baht per person and 20 baht coming down).

Just past the entrance to Chiang Mai Zoo, H 1004 begins to curve and rise and here on the left is a statue commemorating Phra Kru Bha Sri Vichai, the famous monk who, in 1934, initiated the construction of the first proper road up to Doi Suthep so as to make it more accessible to pilgrims.

The road continues to climb (with a few sharp curves) and affords some spectacular views back down over the city. At KM 6.8 a turning on the right leads 3km to Doi Suthep National Park and the small waterfall of Konthathan. Particularly fine views can be seen between KM 9 and 10 while just beyond KM 12 it is possible to catch a glimpse of **Wat Phrathat** perched high up near the summit of the **doi**.

The road reaches the foot of the peak on top of which is the temple. **Wat Phrathat** is approached by a steep flight of 290 steps that leads off from the large parking area lined with food stalls and souvenir shops. The balustrade of the stairway is in the form of **nagas** with brown and green tiles laid to resemble scales.

The site of Wat Phrathat was chosen in the late 14th century when King Ku Na was seeking a repository for holy relics that had been discovered at the same time as those enshrined at Wat Suan Dork. These were placed in a howdah on the back of an elephant which was then set free to wander at will. The beast proceeded to climb Doi Suthep and near the summit it stopped, trumpeted and turned round three times before kneeling down, indicating that this was the chosen spot. The relics were accordingly enshrined in a **chedi**.

The present temple comprising two sanctuaries and cloisters was constructed in the 16th century although the original buildings were several times either added to or restored by later Chiang Mai rulers. The facades of the sanctuaries are superbly decorated and the **chedi**, surrounded by four ornamental umbrellas, is impressively covered with engraved gold plates.

Among the decorations are mural paintings depicting scenes from the lives of the Buddha while the several Buddha images include some fine examples of Chiang Saen and Sukhothai styles. Adding to the overall charm of Wat Phrathat is the mountain perch which it occupies, lending both a distinctive atmosphere and affording magnificent views of the surrounding countryside.

Phuping Palace. From the parking area by the steps to Wat Phrathat the road swings to the left and continues to rise through forests for another 4km to reach Phuping Palace, the summer residence of the Thai Royal Family. The palace buildings are not open to the public but the extensive grounds with their beautifully laid out flower beds (blooms seen best in January) can be viewed Friday to Sunday and on public holidays from 8.30 a.m. to 4.30 p.m. providing no members of the Royal Family are in residence.

The main gates are by KM 18 but the visitor's entrance is 1.2km farther on where there is a parking

Wat Haripunchai, Lamphun

lot on the left and a path on the right leading 200m to the palace grounds.

Meo Village. Some 3km beyond is the Meo village of Ban Doi Pui, reached by a rough track that is often muddy and generally only passable by minibus, truck or jeep, and even then the last stretch must be covered on foot.

The village, although authentic, is far from typical since, due to its proximity to Chiang Mai, it is the most frequently visited of all hilltribe settlements and the Meo here have learnt the price of a photograph and the profits to be made by selling rather poor quality handicrafts (indeed, some of the vendors are not even Meo). Nevertheless, by ignoring the hawkers and the camera posers and wandering deeper into the village it is possible to gain an insight into traditional dress, housing, daily way of life and so forth. Certainly the village should be visited if the traveller does not have time to get to other settlements less affected by the tourist industry.

Wat Chama Devi, Lamphun

Excursion to Lamphun

The historic town of Lamphun, 26km south of Chiang Mai, lies on H 106, known as the Old Chiang Mai Road since, until the Superhighway (H 11) was opened, this was the only link between the northern capital and the main north-south highway (H 1). Public buses plying the route leave Chiang Mai from the terminus on the east bank of the Ping river just across from Nawarat Bridge.

By car, turn right after the bridge onto H 106 which parallels the river. After 600m turn left down Tha Sathoi Road to reach **Wat Tha Sathoi**, the entrance posts of which are distinguished by statues of the elephant-headed deity Ganesha. The facade of the **viharn** has some good gilded woodcarving and the outside is gaily painted bright yellow and red. The eaves of the roof are decorated with **naga** heads and glass inlaid work.

A little beyond is the rear entrance to **Wat San Pakoi** (main entrance for cars on Naipol Road). Of note here is the **bot** which has finely carved doors and decorated pediments. The mural paintings inside the **viharn** are modern but the paintings of guardian figures on the doors and window shutters are quite good although somewhat weathered.

Detour to McKean Institute. A little over 2km from the Tha Sathoi turning, H 1008 forks off right from H 106 to pass Nong Hoy market. Both roads shortly cross H 1141 (airport highway) and a detour along H 1008, which continues to parallel the Ping river, leads to the McKean Rehabilitation Institute for leprosy patients.

About 700m down H 1008 after it has crossed H 1141 is **Wat Chedi Liem** on the left. Here there is a fine Haripunchai-style **chedi** most likely built by King Mengrai at the end of the 13th century and copied from a similar structure at Wat Chama Devi in Lamphun. It is pyramid-shaped with four steps rising to a point and mounted on a square base. Each of the steps has niches on four sides containing Buddha images. The **chedi** was restored in the early 20th century by Phraya Takah, a wealthy resident of Chiang

Mai, who added the lion statues at the corners of the base and the decorative umbrella at the top.

Less than a kilometre away on the right is **Wat Pa Peu** which has a well-carved pediment and in general is typical of Chiang Mai architecture.

One kilometre farther on, a covered gateway to the right leads into the **McKean Institute** (open 8 a.m. to noon and 1 p.m. to 4 p.m. Monday to Friday and mornings only on Saturday). The establishment occupies a small island in the Ping river and covers an area of 160 acres of landscaped grounds. In addition to a clinic and wards for the treatment of leprosy sufferers, there are also physiotherapy and occupational therapy units as well as a church and pleasant residential cottages for the more than 200 in-patients. It is virtually a village unto itself.

The Institute was founded in 1908 by Presbyterian missionary Dr. James W. McKean who developed it to

Umbrella Painting, Bor Sang

become an internationally recognized model of its type. Today, the visitor need have no fear of contagion (the disease is not so fearfully contagious as once thought) and the Institute gives an insight into the valuable work being done and stands as a fascinating testament to the pioneering achievements of Dr. McKean.

Lamphun. From the McKean Institute retrace steps back to H 1141, turn right and then, after 900m, right again to get back on to H 106. This next stretch of the Old Chiang Mai Road is lined on both sides by tall, majestic trees which give a very good idea of what the countryside must have been like before modern development took place.

The highway leads directly into Lamphun, a small town on the right bank of the Kwang river which, since it is now mercifully bypassed by the Superhighway, manages to retain an unhurried charm that otherwise would have long since been lost.

Founded in 660 as the capital of the Mon kingdom of Haripunchai, whose first queen was the legendary Chama Devi, Lamphun remained independent until it was conquered by King Mengrai in 1281 and incorporated into the Lannathai Kingdom. The present town was reconstructed in the early 16th century when it was fortified by walls and a moat; only the latter remains today.

Lamphun is famous for its pretty girls, fine silk weaving (there are several workshops that can be visited) and **lamyai** fruit (in the nearby village of Tonkham there is the so-called '10,000 Baht' **lamyai** tree which supposedly annually nets its owner that value of fruit, although probably more at today's prices). More importantly, two of the city's temples are major attractions, one being among the finest in the North and the other possessing two exceptionally well-preserved ancient **chedis.**

Wat Phra That Haripunchai ranks supreme in terms of architectural beauty and historical interest and should be at the top of any sightseeing list. The compound backs on to H 106 as you enter the town and a left turn should be made to approach it via the main entrance which faces the river.

The temple was built in 1044 by King Athitayaraj, the 32nd ruler of Haripunchai, on the site of the former royal palace. Two red/brown ornamental lions guard the gateway next to which is a **bot**, unfortunately generally kept locked although containing two fine bronze Buddha statues seated beneath a canopy in the shape of a spire.

First encountered inside the compound is the modern **viharn** which, although built in 1925 (the original being destroyed by fire in 1915), is nevertheless constructed in the traditional style with a three-tiered, low-sloping roof and deep porticos. It houses a large Chiang Saen-style bronze Buddha, **Phra Chao Thongtip**, plus a number of smaller images. To the left of the altar are beautifully carved **thammas** and two rather over-ornate gilded thrones. Mural paintings above the doorway and inside depict scenes from the lives of the Buddha although they possess no great artistic value.

Outside the **viharn** to the left is a Lannathai-style manuscript repository dating from the early 19th century and containing religious texts in the northern style along with accounts of local history. To the right of the **viharn** is a giant bronze gong cast in 1860 and claimed to be the world's largest.

In the centre of the compound is an imposing 50m-high Chiang Saen-style **chedi** covered in copper plates and topped by a gold umbrella. Surrounded by railings, it is the most sacred part of the temple and also the oldest with construction having begun in 897 while later additions were to raise it to its present height.

To the right and slightly behind the main **chedi** is a stepped pyramid **chedi**, known as **Suwanna Chedi**, built four years after its larger counterpart and copied from a design seen at Wat Chama Devi. To the north is another **chedi** in Chiang Saen-style and named **Chedi Mae Krua**.

In the rear of the compound is a **viharn** enshrining the standing Buddha known as **Phra Chao Tan Jai** and nearby is the old museum and a **sala** housing four Buddha footprints one inside the other **(Phrabat Si Roi).**

The **new museum**, located outside the temple compound on the opposite side of the main road, is the perfect adjunct to a visit to Wat Phra That Haripunchai and should not be missed. It is small but extremely well laid out and contains a valuable collection of exhibits including bronze, stone and stucco statues from various periods together with examples of woodcarving and other decorative items. Of special note are the superb Dvaravati stucco work dating from the 7th to the late 9th centuries and fragments of a rare silver Buddha image.

Wat Chama Devi, (also known as **Wat Ku Kut**), is Lamphun's second most important temple lying beyond the moat on the western side of town, 1km down the road leading to Sanpathong village. It was founded by the 2nd ruler of Haripunchai, King Mahantayot, on the death of his mother, Queen Chama Devi, in 715. The main temple buildings seen today are modern but the interest lies in the two old **chedis.**

The largest, **Suwan Chang Kot**, on the right after the entrance, dates from the 8th century — well restored in 1964 — and is an excellent example of the late Dvaravati style. Made of laterite, it is in the form of

Chiang Mai Silversmiths

a five-step pyramid 21m high and 15.35m wide at the base. Each of the steps has niches on the four sides containing standing Buddhas.

To the left is the smaller (11.5m high) brick-built, octagonal-shaped **Ratana Chedi** which was most likely first constructed in the 10th century but rebuilt in the 12th by King Phaya Sapphasit. (It was restored in 1967.) Again, standing Buddhas in niches decorate the first step of the structure.

Also worth visiting is **Wat Phra Yeun** which is located about 1km from Lamphun centre across the Kwang river on the road to Lampang. It is noted for its Burmese-style **chedi**, shaped like a **mondop** and rebuilt in 1900 on the site of a **mondop** constructed by King Ku Na of Chiang Mai in 1369 to shelter four standing Buddha statues.

Pa Sang, 12km from Lamphun along H 106, is a small, basically one-street town noted for cotton weaving, batik, **lamyai** and girls who some say are even more attractive than those of Lamphun. It was founded by Phraya Kawila after Chiang Mai had been liberated from Burmese control in the 18th century. The town's unaltered way of life is its main attraction although at **Wat Pa Sang Ngam**, in the main street, there is an interesting manuscript repository dating from the beginning of the Rattanakosin (Bangkok) period.

Karen Village. A few kilometres to the east between Lamphun and Pa Sang is a sizeable settlement of Karen hilltribe people set amid lush rice fields. Named **Ban Mae Kanard Luang**, the village can be reached from Lamphun as follows: at KM 149.5 (this is the distance from the Thoen end of the road, not Chiang Mai) on H 106, turn left on to H 1033 (along this road are villages noted for making hats out of dried palm leaves). After KM 8 the road crosses H 16, and then 800m past KM 15 it swings to the left while the right-hand fork (surfaced only in parts) leads through the village of Thambol Thakad. Turn left 1.5km beyond the village and then left again along a narrow dirt track through rice fields and after 1.3km fork right to enter the Karen village.

Excursion to Bor Sang & San Kamphaeng

The road from Chiang Mai to the handicraft villages of Bor Sang and San Kamphaeng is something of a shopper's 'Golden Mile' (or rather golden 13 kilometres). The way is lined with numerous factories/shops producing a variety of handicrafts and where it is possible to see craftsmen at work as well as purchase finished products. Chiang Mai's famous handicrafts and shopping prospects are described more fully in the following section but the excursion outlined here can be just as much a shopping spree as a sightseeing trip.

The journey follows H 1006 which runs east of the city from Nawarat Bridge. Among the many handicraft establishments in the 6km stretch after the road crosses the Superhighway are: 'Chiang Mai Tusnaporn Company' (woodcarving and teak centre plus a separate showroom for antique Buddhas and blue and white ceramics); 'Silver Making Centre'; 'Sadaluk Carving'; 'Chiang Mai Treasure' (woodcarving) and 'Saithong Antiques & Handicraft' (a good collection of items displayed in typical northern-style houses).

Bor Sang. A few hundred metres past 'Saithong Antiques' is a turning on the left (H 1014) that leads into Bor Sang (9km from Chiang Mai), the village

Night Market, Chiang Mai

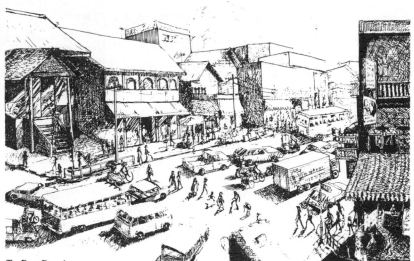

Ta Pae Road, Chiang Mai

famous for umbrella-making. The umbrellas are traditionally made out of a split bamboo frame and hand-made paper covers (today cotton and rayon fabrics are also used). The popularity of the craft has declined somewhat in recent years but there are still a number of workshops (the largest being 'Umbrella Making Centre' on the right just after the turnoff) where the whole process can be seen. The work most fascinating to watch is the painting of the covers by young girls who use a single brush with two colours and with a few deft flicks of the wrist manage to create beautiful floral patterns.

In an effort to promote Bor Sang and help revive interest in the flagging umbrella industry, a three-day 'Umbrella Festival' was held in December 1982 and it is hoped that this will become an annual event. Highlights include parades with elephants, and girls holding umbrellas, umbrella dancing and, of course, a beauty contest.

Detour to Doi Saket. 14km beyond Bor Sang along H 1014 is the locally popular beauty spot of Doi Saket. The **doi** (a small hill in this case and not a mountain) has a flight of steps leading to a temple at the top, although the attraction of the climb lies less in the building than in the fine views of the surrounding lush countryside. Just under 2km to the left around the base of the hill leads to the pretty lotus pond of **Nong Bua**, a tranquil spot where there are a couple of small restaurants.

Passing close to Doi Saket is H 1019 (the new Chiang Rai road) which leads directly back to Chiang Mai.

San Kamphaeng. Continuing on from the Bor Sang turnoff, H 1006 passes several more handicraft centres — notably 'Boon Lacquerware'; 'Siam Celadon'; 'Silk Farm & Weaving' and 'Thai-Burma Tribal Craft' — before entering the important silk and cotton weaving centre of San Kamphaeng some 4km away.

This township has long been famous for the quality of its silk and cotton and there are many workshops where girls can be seen weaving cloth on primitive hand looms. Two of the largest weaving concerns are 'Piankusol Weaving' and 'Shinawa Ra Panich,' both on the left side of the road as you enter the town.

Cooperative Village & Muang On Cave. At the crossroads in San Kamphaeng the left-hand turning leads 11km to San Kamphaeng Cooperative Village, established by Royal Command in 1976. This largish cooperative gives a good impression of typical rural life and offers some attractive scenery. Currently there are plans to develop and promote the area, which includes nearby hot springs, as a tourist attraction.

About 5km beyond the village is **Muang On Cave** situated on a hill and reached by a flight of steps. By the entrance is a small **chedi** built to commemorate Phra Kru Bha Sri Vichai (the monk famous for building the road up to Doi Suthep). Inside, a long flight of steps leads down into the heart of the cave where there is a statue of the sleeping Buddha and a large chamber with a 4m high limestone formation and, close by, a seated Buddha image.

Other Short Excursions

Several other interesting destinations that can be covered in half- and full-day trips from Chiang Mai have been included in the longer itineraries described elsewhere in this book. Most popular among these are:

Doi Inthanon & Mae Klang Waterfall (P.57)

Mae Sa Valley — picturesque scenery, waterfall and elephant camp. (P.75)

Chiang Dao Cave (P.80)

Lampang — interesting temples and only town in Thailand still having horse-drawn carriages. (P.108)

Lampang Young Elephant Training Centre (P.107)

Handicrafts & Shopping

Chiang Mai could well lay claim to being the world's largest centre for cottage industries. Despite the economic developments that have taken place in recent years, there are still a number of communities living in and around the city practising a variety of handicraft trades that have been family occupations for centuries. Add to these traditional local products antiques from Burma and hilltribe handicrafts (especially silver jewellery and embroidery work) and Chiang Mai becomes a veritable shopper's paradise.

Even if the traveller is not especially attracted by the idea of bargain hunting, at least some of the workshops should be visited to see craftsmen at work at their time-honoured trades, using tools and techniques that have changed little over the years.

Listed below are some of the best buys along with indications of the main shopping areas. For names and addresses of recommended shops, however, the traveller is advised to obtain a free copy of the 'Official Shopping Guide' published by the Tourism Authority of Thailand. And, remember that apart from in the modern shops where prices are fixed, bargaining is still the rule when shopping. It takes a little time and patience but it is all part of the experience.

Silk & Cotton. Handwoven silks and cottons in delightful colours are among Thailand's best known products and can be purchased either by the length or made up into dresses, shirts etc. The finest quality silk is made at San Kamphaeng while Lamphun and nearby Pa Sang are also noted for their silk and, more especially, cotton weaving.

Woodcarving. Teak wood is indigenous to northern Thailand and formerly ranked among the country's leading export commodities. Today, the forests are becoming depleted and teak is now one of the most expensive woods. Nevertheless, the old craft of woodcarving still thrives in Chiang Mai and good quality, richly carved furniture can be obtained at most favourable prices. Among more transportable items are trays, salad bowls and carved figures of people and animals (elephants are understandably common although it is hard to fathom what anyone would do with some of the giant statues almost the size of a real life baby pachyderm!). A number of good woodcarving shops are located on Raj Chiang Saen Road near Chiang Mai Gate.

Silverware. Chiang Mai's old community of silversmiths is centred on Wualai Road which runs south-west from Chiang Mai Gate. Craftsmen in numerous workshops here produce a variety of items but most famous are the silver bowls with highly intricate hammered designs, often depicting scenes from the 'Ramayana' epic or from the lives of the Buddha. The silver used is close to 100% pure and the metal is accordingly light in both colour and weight.

Silver jewellery is another popular buy in Chiang Mai, much of it made by hilltribe craftsmen. Rings, necklaces, earrings and bracelets are common and often chunky in design. Note that the quality of the metal should be carefully checked as the silver content is, in some cases, less than what is claimed.

Lacquerware. Another thriving cottage industry is lacquerware, items made from applying several layers of resin over a bamboo frame which, when hardened is polished to a high gloss and painted. The craft has strong Burmese influences and, indeed, many of the pieces for sale do come from that neighbouring country. Boxes, chests, trays, small tables and decorative plates are available with traditional colours being black and gold or orange, green and yellow. Lacquerware workshops and showrooms can be found in particular along Wualai Road close to the silversmiths' community.

Celadon Pottery. Ever since King Ramkamhaeng settled Chinese potters at Sukhothai and Si Stachanalai in the late 13th century, northern Thailand has been famous for its ceramics. The producers of what was then known as Sawankhalok pottery moved north to the town of San Kamphaeng after the collapse of the Sukhothai Kingdom and their craft continued to flourish there for some time until eventually falling into decline. In recent years, however, efforts have been made to revive the industry and Celadon pottery is now produced, following largely the techniques employed by the Sawankhalok craftsmen. There are currently four major ceramic factories in the Chiang Mai area, the best known being 'Thai Celadon Company' whose factory is located on the Fang road (H 107) near KM 6. A wide variety of products are available — vases, figurines, ashtrays, lamp bases etc.

Umbrellas. The production of hand-painted umbrellas made out of bamboo and paper is the traditional cottage industry of the village of Bor Sang (see P.40)

Other recommended buys include jewellery made from 24kt gold-plated orchids; high quality leather goods in a variety of skins and hilltribe embroidery and costumes. Antiques and objects d'art, mostly smuggled in from Burma, are also fairly common although certain pieces will require export certificates which should be provided by the shop concerned. Some genuine articles are certainly available although good judgement is required when shopping, since the production of 'instant antiques' is a latter day cottage industry.

Shopping Centres & Markets

Ta Pae Road has for long been Chiang Mai's principal shopping centre and most things can still be found here. However, with the expansion of the city, this main thoroughfare no longer has a monopoly and shops and businesses are increasingly spreading throughout the central area.

Night Bazaar. A fascinating place for browsing and picking up hilltribe handicrafts and many types of low-priced souvenirs is the Night Bazaar on Chang Klan Road in front of the Chiang Inn hotel. Formerly a ramshackle sprawl of make-shift stalls, the bazaar has now been housed in a new covered area built in mock northern style. Business generally gets going around 6 p.m.

Markets. Chiang Mai's traditional markets are also

worth a visit although perhaps more for seeing how the locals shop, than for making actual purchases.

Warorot Market, at the intersection of Chang Moi and Wichayanon roads, is a bustling place and, covering three storeys, it is the city's largest fresh produce market as well as being the principal store for household goods, clothing, cosmetics etc. **Suan Buak Hat**, by Suan Prung Gate, is the main flower market and presents a colourful display. At **Somphet Market**, which borders the moat in the northeast corner of the city near the junction with Chang Moi Road, can be seen all the varieties of fresh fruit for which the North is famous.

Dining Out

Considering its size, Chiang Mai offers a remarkable selection of dining possibilities. There is a wide variety of types of cuisine available and restaurants ranging from the fairly expensive, elegant establishments to the cheap but good local street stalls.

Described below are the major cuisines and some of the better known places where they are obtainable. The list is representative but not exhaustive and, moreover, it is taken for granted that the city's major hotels have excellent restaurants but by no means a monopoly on fine dining. Outside the top hotels, the average price for a meal for two (excluding drinks) would be around 300 baht and considerably less in small Thai restaurants.

Northern Thai Food

The typical cuisine of northern Thailand is distinct from that of the rest of the country being largely influenced by Burmese recipes — one of the lasting traces of the historical invaders — and is most notably characterised by its spicy curries.

The best introduction to Northern food is a **khantoke** dinner, the traditional fare for entertaining important guests. **Khan** literally means 'bowl' and **toke** is a small, low round table usually made of rattan or lacquerware, around which diners sit on the floor and share a number of dishes that are taken together with sticky rice, another speciality of the North, as well as plain rice.

The principal dishes of a **khantoke** dinner are:

Kaeng Hang Le: pork curry with garlic, ginger and other spices.

Namprik Ong: minced pork cooked with tomato, cucumber, onion and chilies.

Cap Moo: fried pork skin.

Kang Kai: chicken and vegetable curry.

Larb: minced meat mixed with chilies and taken with various kinds of vegetables.

Today, entertainment has become another essential ingredient of **khantoke** dinners and they are usually accompanied by performances of traditional northern dances such as **Fon Leb** (fingernail dance) and **Rum Fad Khao** (rice winnowing dance). Hilltribe dances are also often presented.

The two places where **khantoke** dinner is a speciality in Chiang Mai are: **Old Chiang Mai Cultural Centre**, 185/3 Wualai Road. Tel: 235097. (Here there are also resident hilltribe people who live in reconstructed typical tribal houses within the grounds thus giving a potted introduction to the culture of the various tribes.)

Diamond Hotel, 33/10 Charoenprathet Road. Tel: 234153, 234155.

Dinners at both places commence at 7 p.m. and are priced at 180 baht per head, exclusive of drinks but including transfers from/to hotel.

A few other northern delicacies apart from **khantoke** specialities are: **tabong** (bamboo shoots boiled then fried in batter); **sai owa** (sausage filled with minced pork mixed with herbs) and **jing kung** (an insect similar to a cricket — now rare and generally only available at Arun Rai restaurant, see below).

Restaurant Selection

THAI

Baan Suan, 51/3 Chiang Mai San Kamphaeng Road. Tel: 234116. Excellent food and pleasant setting in typical northern-style teak house. Specialities include Fried Shrimp with Chili Paste (hot!); Pork Curry Burmese Style; Chiang Mai Sausage; Grilled Black Fish and Grilled Spare Ribs.

Arun Rai, 45 Kojchasarn Road. Generally only place where **jing kung** is available. Also good curries and Chinese dishes.

Galae Restaurant, Northern Agricultural Development Centre, 65 Suthep Road. Good food and superb setting, partly in open air, on tree-shaded hill overlooking reservoir.

Kaiwan, 181 Nimman Hemin Road. Tel: 222147, 221687.

CHINESE

Today Restaurant, 90/2 Viang Ping Bazaar, Chang Klan Road. Tel: 236251. Dim Sum luncheon only.

Canton Suki, 97/100 Huai Kaeo Road.

VEGETARIAN

Mang Sa Virat, 11 Suthep Road. Open for lunch only. Inexpensive.

Whole Earth, 88 Sridonchai Road. Tel: 232463. Indian and Thai vegetarian dishes.

Sawaeng Tadthieng (Farmer Sawaeng), 214 Kilometre 5, Chiang Mai — Doi Saket Road, Sansai Noi, Amphur Sansai. Not strictly vegetarian but renowned for its fresh vegetables. Superb crispy salads a speciality. Garden setting.

SEAFOOD

Nang Nual Seafood, 27/2-5 Koa Klang Road, Nong Hoi. Tel: 235771, 232274. Sister restaurant to one of same name in Pattaya. Excellent food (including Japanese dishes); pleasant landscaped grounds with bird garden, waterfall and shopping arcade. Selection of dining rooms.

JAPANESE

Tokugawa, Chiang Mai Hills Hotel, 18 Huai Kaeo Road. Tel: 221254-5.

JUNGLE FOOD

Charueng Rueng, 5 Superhighway (Airport Road). On banks of Ping river. Cobra and mongoose among the unusual dishes served. Caged bears and snake pit outside. Run by ex-army sergeant who has put his jungle survival training to profitable use.

FRENCH

Le Coq d'Or, 18-20 Chaiyapoom Road. Excellent French and Continental cuisine. Fireside, old world setting.

The Chalet, 71 Charoenprathet Road. Tel: Tel: 236810. Located in old northern-style teak house.

ITALIAN

Babylon Restaurant, 100/63 Huai Kaeo Road. Good selection of Italian specialities at very reasonable prices. Ground floor not especially inviting but pleasant dining rooms on two upper storeys.

GERMAN

Haus Munchen, 115/3 Loi Kroa Road. Typical German fare plus draft beer.

ENGLISH

The Pub, 88 Huai Kaeo Road. Good Western specialities in typical Thai house miraculously given the atmosphere of an English country pub that is surprisingly authentic, given that the pub concept does not travel well. Friendly and cosy; good place for meeting expatriate residents.

PAKISTANI, INDIAN & ARABIC

Al-Shiraz, 123-123/1 Chang Klan Road (opposite Night Bazaar). Tel: 234338. Tandoori Chicken; Mutton, Chicken & Prawn Biriani; Mutton & Chicken Tikka; Seekh Kebab etc.

BUDGET & BREAKFAST

There are a number of small establishments serving American breakfasts and budget meals. Among the best known are: **Thai-German Dairy**, 33 Moon Muang Road; **Daret Restaurant**, 59/63 Moon Muang Road and **Galare Guesthouse**, 7-7/1 Charoenprathet Road.

FOOD STALLS

Chiang Mai is dotted with areas where food stalls cluster, especially at night. Good basic Thai food; tables and stools on sidewalk permitting view of ever-changing street scene. Small local restaurants and food stalls are common at: Chang Klan Road near the Night Bazaar and around Ta Pae, White Elephant and Chiang Mai Gates.

NIGHTLIFE

Bangkok's reputation for exciting nightlife is not shared by Chiang Mai. There are, for example, no specific bar areas and no go-go bars. However, one of the results of modern development is that the city is no longer moribund once the sun has set.

In the main, nighttime entertainment ranges from disco to large, Thai-style nightclubs, smaller bar/lounges with live music and massage parlours. Most nightspots get underway around 8 p.m. while massage parlours are open from 6 p.m. to midnight on weekdays and from 2 p.m. to midnight on weekends and public holidays. The following is a brief selection of after dark choices.

DISCO

Byblos Disco Club, Rincome Hotel, 310 Huai Kaeo Road. Recorded music.

Club 77, Orchid Hotel, 100-2 Huai Kaeo Road. Recorded music.

Pornping Disco, Pornping Hotel, 46-48 Charoenprathet Road. Live band.

NIGHTCLUBS

Thai-style with live band, dancing partners, food

and drink. Generally large establishments with little in the way of an intimate atmosphere.

Blue Moon, 5/3 Moon Muang Road.

Hennessy, Muang Mai Hotel, 502 Huai Kaeo Road.

Bunny Playboy Club, 198 Tippanetr Road.

Rin Kaeo, Chotana Road near Mahakorn Road.

Honey Chiangmai, 595 Superhighway. Large entertainment centre.

BARS/MUSIC LOUNGES

Cellar Folk & Music Pub, Prince Hotel, 3 Taiwang Road. Country & Western.

Harmony, Huai Kaeo Road (opposite Orchid Hotel). Small but cosy and sophisticated. Good classical guitar, violin and piano music.

Jazz Inn, 99/10 Huai Kaeo Road (next to Rintr Hotel).

Karen Hut, 13 Changmoi Road (behind Le Coq d'Or restaurant). Hostesses and solo guitar player. Perhaps the most popular nightspot for the single male.

The Pub, 88 Huai Kaeo Road. English pub atmosphere.

Ship Cafe, 21/1 Jaroenrat Road. Live music.

Sweet Room, 38/4 Rajawithi Road. Live music.

MASSAGE PARLOURS

Atami, 92 Chaiyapoom Road (opposite Somphet Market).

Chiang Mai Hills Hotel, 18 Huai Kaeo Road.

Chiangmai Massage, next to Chiang Inn Hotel.

Ginza, Manee Noparat Road (next to Tantrapan Supermarket).

Sayuri, 3 Soi 2 Bumrungrat Road.

Muang Mai Hotel, 502 Huai Kaeo Road.

CINEMAS

Because of high import tax few Western movies are shown and programmes are usually confined to Thai-made films.

Fathani, Muang Mai Shopping Centre, Huai Kaeo Road.

Muang Fah, Wangsingkham Road.
Nakorn Chiangmai, Chotana Road.
Saengtawan, 5/4 Chang Klan Road.
Suriwongse, 15 Kotchasarn Road.
Suriya, Kotchasarn Road.
Suriyong, Loy Kroh Road.
Tippanetr Rama, Tippanetr Shopping Centre.

VIDEO MOVIES

Several hotels and bars show reasonably recent movies in video form with original soundtrack. They include:
Cellar, Prince Hotel, 3 Taiwang Road.
Chiang Inn Hotel, Chang Klan Road.
Chiangmai Palace, Chang Klan Road.
Karen Hut, 13 Changmoi Road.
Chiang Mai Hills Hotel, 18 Huai Kaeo Road.
Oasis Bar, Rajmankla Soi 2 (off Moon Muang Road).
Ship Cafe, 21/1 Jaroenrat Road.

NIGHTTIME COMPANIONS

For a nighttime companion the single male need only ask a friendly trishaw driver and be pedalled away to find the girl of his choice. Settle price in advance. The risks are the same as anywhere else.

CHIANG MAI TO MAE HONG SON

Mae Hong Son, close to the Burmese border northwest of Chiang Mai, has been jokingly referred to as the 'former Siberia of Thailand'. The label does not relate to any climate parallel between this part of the country and East Russia, but rather to the fact that the town, like Siberia, was once a favoured spot for exiling disgraced or unwanted politicians and officials.

Until comparatively recently Mae Hong Son was virtually cut off from the rest of Thailand. Tucked away in a forgotten corner and hemmed in by mountains, it was accessible only by a long and difficult trek on elephant back. Not until 1965 was a paved road opened linking the town with Chiang Mai.

Of course, no one is exiled today, yet Mae Hong Son retains an air of separate development and still manages to exude a sleepy old-world charm entirely its own. The surprise for the modern traveller is that the former place of exile, far from being grim, is like Shangri-la, an enchanting, lush hidden valley.

Mae Hong Son is now easily reached from Chiang Mai by the daily Thai Airways flight — a mere 30-minute hop over the mountains. The journey by road is quite a different proposition. Highway 108 heads first southward from Chiang Mai to Hot and then, completing a broad horseshoe curve, west to Mae Sariang and from there north to Mae Hong Son, a total distance of 369km.

The flight is ideal for those in a hurry but for others with more time to spare the road trip is recommended. Not only do a number of interesting places lie en route, but also the mountain scenery is some of the finest in all Thailand and makes the drive an experience in itself.

As mentioned, H 108 was opened in 1965 and is quite an engineering feat. At one point (Ban Ton Ngew) it is the highest road in the country at 1,513m above sea level and such is the rugged terrain it traverses that construction costs (at current exchange rates) averaged US$69,000 per km, rising at the most difficult spots to US$177,000 per km. During the construction of the road, six workers were killed in a blasting accident in 1958 and a small memorial now stands by the roadside at KM 24 beyond Hot.

There are five buses a day from Chiang Mai to Mae Hong Son (the earliest leaving at 6.30 a.m.) and the journey takes about 10 hours. By car, the distance can be covered in roughly eight hours but if the places of interest en route are to be visited, it is best to break the journey and overnight in Mae Sariang where there is one reasonable hotel, the Mitaree.

To join H 108, leave Chiang Mai by the gate of the same name and head southwest on Wualai Road which leads into H 108 after crossing the airport highway (1141).

CITY MAP OF MAE HONG SON

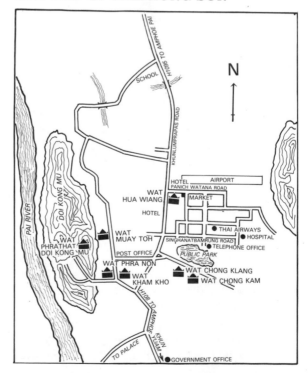

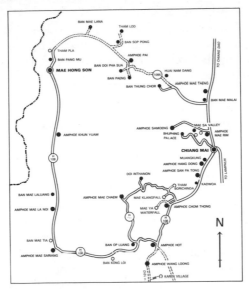

ROUTE MAP:
CHIANG MAI TO MAE HONG SON

On the outskirts of the city there is little of interest other than a small celadon factory and some lacquerware workshops on the left about 4km from Chiang Mai Gate. However, 8km from the city there is an interesting old teak rice storage house on the left side of the road. It is raised up on stilts and has carved wooden sides and roof; although no longer used, it is preserved by its owner as an antique.

Pottery Village. A dirt track on the right just after KM 10 leads directly into the tiny village of **Muangkung**. Virtually the entire population here is engaged in pottery making — pots for household use, not souvenirs — and the practice of this traditional craft can be seen by strolling around the 50-odd wooden houses. Each house is built up on stilts and the craftsmen huddle in the area below, shaping the clay on primitive wheels. The natural light brown clay is given its characteristic reddish hue by mixing it with iron minerals, or else it is blackened by mixing with charcoal from the kilns. One thing to note about the houses is at the entrance to most there is a pole supporting a water bowl and ladle; drinking water that is traditionally made available to travellers in the North.

Despite the proximity of Chiang Mai, life at Muangkung has been little affected by the city and the village is rarely visited by tourists. Accordingly, this quiet spot gives a vivid impression of old fashioned village life.

A couple of kilometres farther along H 108 is the village of Hang Dong which is noted for its bamboo weaving and a number of shops selling baskets and other items line both sides of the road.

The highway continues to pass through the flat fertile plain, passing now and then, small hamlets. There is little of interest along this stretch except, 2km beyond Amphoe San Pa Tong, wooden pens on the right mark the site of the **kadwoa** or cattle market. This is held only on Saturday mornings and, should the traveller be passing at this time, a brief stop is worthwhile as the market is a lively affair with not only livestock and agricultural equipment for sale but also just about everything else from Levis to motorbikes.

Mae Klang Waterfall

Doi Inthanon and Mae Klang Waterfall. Around KM 34 Doi Inthanon, Thailand's highest mountain at 2,565 m, can be glimpsed in the distance off to the right. It is an elongated mountain and as such belies its true height. The turnoff to Doi Inthanon National Park and Mae Klang Waterfall is just before KM 57 and is signposted in Thai and English — 8km to the waterfall and 48km to the top of the mountain.

One kilometre along the Doi Inthanon road is a turning on the left that leads 14km to **Mae Ya** waterfall. However, although it starts off paved, the side road soon deteriorates into an unsurfaced, and in parts steep, trail impassable by ordinary car. The waterfall can nevertheless be glimpsed in the distance, appearing as a white splash against the green hillside.

Six kilometres farther on, the road forks; to the right leads to the top of the mountain (a good paved road all the way) while to the left is Mae Klang waterfall.

There is a toll levied on all vehicles making the trip up Doi Inthanon — 50 baht for minibuses, 20 baht for cars and 5 baht for motorbikes. At the top there is a radar station while on the way up lie first Wachiratarn and later Siriphum waterfalls. Beautiful scenery, birds, flowers and spectacular views all make the excursion well worthwhile. It is possible to camp on the mountainside although only if permission has been obtained in advance from the Forestry Department in Bangkok.

If travelling by public transport, both Doi Inthanon and Mae Ya waterfall can be visited by taking the bus from Chiang Mai to Chom Thong where minibus trucks can be hired for around 550-600 baht for the round trip. Each truck takes 6-8 passengers.

One kilometre along the left-hand fork by the foot of Doi Inthanon is Mae Klang waterfall. There is a parking lot on the left surrounded by food stalls from where it is a 20 m walk to the falls. Entrance fee: adults 3 baht, children 1 baht.

Mae Klang is a picturesque spot and is a popular picnic area with the people of Chiang Mai. The water tumbles impressively 29 m over three rocky ledges while a footpath leads up a short distance to a higher level, Pakan Na falls, which are broader but less steep than Mae Klang.

For the energetic, the footpath continues farther up the hillside and affords some fine views. There is also a cave, **Tham Borichinda**, in the vicinity but as it is more than one hour's trek away it is only of interest to the dedicated speleologist. To get there it is necessary to obtain the services of a guide or a rough sketch map from the Forestry Department office by the entrance to Mae Klang.

Chom Thong. One kilometre beyond the Doi Inthanon turnoff H 108 enters the small town of Chom Thong. The place has little to recommend itself other than **Wat Phra That Si Chom Thong** which is located on the left of the main road in the town centre.

Directly inside the main gate is an old Burmese-style **chedi** dating from 1451 while to the right, behind a modern **chedi**, is a venerable bo tree, its branches supported by many props placed there by devotees. Despite the seeming anachronism of the new **chedi**, the first impression created by the compound is one of taking a step back in time. The feeling is enhanced by the temple building itself.

The **viharn**, built by King Muang Keo in 1516, is a graceful old building distinguished by a two-tiered roof with gables and facades decorated with intricate woodcarving. Inside, 10 sturdy pillars support the roof

Karen Hilltribe Women

Ob Luang Gorge

and the interior is dominated by a tall, highly ornate
mondop prasart which enshrines a Buddha relic.
Surrounding the **mondop prasart** are some exquisite
Buddha statues and carved elephant tusks.

Behind are two iron-barred glass cabinets, the one on
the left containing small gold Buddha statues and the
other housing silver and crystal Buddhas and other
artifacts decorated with precious stones. At the
opposite end of the **viharn** is a glass case holding some
antique weapons.

Outside the **viharn** is a long wooden trough leading
to a small gated and roofed shrine where the holy relic
is placed during the Songkran festival and devotees
pay their respects by pouring water over it by means of
the curious trough device.

From Chom Thong H 108 crosses the Mae Klang
river by KM 63 and 1km farther on, the Ping river
comes into sight and parallels the left side of the road
which follows the valley southward to Hot. The scenery
now begins to get more interesting with low forested
hills in the background and a profusion of trees in the
foreground, their many hues of green broken here and
there by the red outbursts of flame trees.

Hot. The small town of Hot, 88km from Chiang Mai,
was formerly sited 15km farther downstream on the
Ping river but was re-located some years ago when the
land became submerged by the formation of the
reservoir following the construction of Bhumipol Dam

(see p.145). This fact is reflected in the appearance of the present-day settlement which is an unattractive collection of seemingly hurriedly constructed shophouses strung out along both sides of the main road. There is nothing of interest in the town although it is a convenient place to stop and take a simple meal. The few Karen tribespeople in from the countryside on a shopping spree add a touch of colour to this otherwise drab town.

On the far outskirts of Hot, H 108 swings to the right while H 1012 continues straight on towards Doi Tao and Wang Lung.

Doi Tao. One kilometre down H 1012 a turning on the left (H 1103) leads 33km to the settlement of Doi Tao, on the banks of the Mae Ping lake. There are a few floating bungalows on the lake a short distance from the village and these, offering basic accommodation, can be rented from Ta-Pae Bannakarn bookshop in Ta Pae Road, Chiang Mai (bookings must be made at least one week in advance).

Ob Luang Gorge

Mae Ping is a picturesque lake and rafts or longtail boats can be hired for the 140km trip down to Bhumipol Dam. Alternatively, Chiang Mai Lake Tour company charters two large vessels — accommodating 50 and 100 passengers respectively — for the same journey which takes in places of interest en route, such as the waterfall at Arb Nang cliff and the ruins of the old abandoned town of Muang Soi. Charters (booked at least one month in advance) from Doi Tao to Bhumipol Dam cost 9,000 baht one way or 12,000 baht roundtrip and may be booked at Chiang Mai Lake Tour Co. Ltd., 97-99 Charoenmuang Road, Chiang Mai, or 61/1 Soi Lang Suan, Ploenchit Road, Bangkok.

Wang Lung. Continuing straight on from the Doi Tao turnoff, H 1012 soon deteriorates into a laterite track. On either side of the road can be spotted a few ruined **chedis**, all that remain of the ancient town of Hot, while 10km from the turnoff is a giant stone seated Buddha on the left. Four kilometres farther on, H 1012 reaches the fishing village of Wang Lung. This once popular little place, noted for its dried fish, has fallen on hard times since successive years of poor rains have resulted in a drop in the water level of the lake and it is no longer possible to hire boats as was formerly the case.

Karen Village. According to the maps, H 1012 ends at Wang Lung but in fact a track continues for another 5km to the Huai Mae Kho Rua river, a few hundred metres beyond which lies the Karen village of Ban Huai Fang. In the dry season the small river can be forded by car; at other times it is necessary to wade across and walk to the settlement.

Ban Huai Fang is a large Karen village comprising some 100 houses built on stilts and around 500 inhabitants. Because of its relative isolation it is mostly unaffected by modern-day developments and women can be seen working at primitive hand looms, weaving their traditional cloth. During the day, however, the place is generally quiet as the men are away in the fields cultivating soya beans and peanuts.

From Ban Huai Fang it is necessary to retrace one's steps back along H 1012 before turning left on to H 108 once more. Teak trees, with their distinctive broad leaves now join the mass of greenery bordering the road and 3km beyond Hot H 108 comes to parallel the Chaem river on the right before beginning its ups and downs through the hills that turn the journey west to Mae Sariang into something of a roller-coaster ride.

Ob Luang Gorge. Off to the right of the road 17km from Hot is Ob Luang Gorge, occasionally outrageously mis-described as Thailand's answer to the Grand Canyon. In reality it is nothing like it but the steep, narrow gorge, its walls almost meeting at the top, is nevertheless an intriguing sight. It is spanned by a rickety wooden bridge from where you can look down at the waters of the Chaem river hurtling through the narrows 50m below.

Steps lead down from the roadside to the bridge, or a few metres farther on, there is a turning to the right into Ob Luang Nature Park where you can park the car and walk 200m to the bottom of the gorge. The picturesque scenery is enhanced by an abundance of colourful birds and butterflies.

Wat Utthayarom, Mae Sariang

Rice Threshing

Hot Springs. Five kilometres along H 108 from Ob Luang Gorge is a turning on the right for H 1088, an unsurfaced road that leads to the settlement of Mae Chaem. After a bone-shaking 10 km drive along this track you arrive at the hot sulphur springs of **Thepanom Mineral Well.**

The springs, some at temperatures of 99°C, bubble out of the ground at various spots in a kind of rocky meadow crossed by steaming little streams; a light smell of sulphur permeates the air. Some picnic tables and barbecue sites have been laid out although the place is generally deserted and, to be truthful, a visit to the springs is only really worthwhile for those with a keen interest in such places.

H 108 now rises steadily to a plateau through a series of undulations and the views of the mountains on either side are magnificent. Suddenly pine trees appear in profusion, turning the scenery into something more reminiscent of Scandinavia than Thailand. It is in this area that the government is experimenting with the cultivation of pine trees in an effort to stem the deforestation caused by the destructive slash-and-burn farming technique of the hilltribes. This denuding of the hillsides of their natural vegetation — which causes soil erosion and the destruction of watersheds — can be seen in many places along the way to Mae Sariang where whole hillsides appear as if a giant razor has been passed over and only a few charred tree stumps, like stubble, remain to remind one of the forest that once was.

Pine trees have been chosen as they are faster growing than the indigenous teak and the wood has a number of uses, notably in paper-making. At **Baw Keow Nursery**, 14km from the H 1088 turnoff, young pine trees can be seen on the left planted out in neat rows rather like a rubber plantation. Another 15km along H 108, on the right, is the entrance to the **Pine Improvement Centre**, a Thai-Danish co-project for the propagation of pine forests. In between these two places the highway passes the Lawa village of **Bor Luang** and frequently along the way tribespeople can be seen by the roadside.

H 108 becomes increasingly exciting as the region gets more hilly and by KM 39 there is a superb 2km stretch where the road takes on the aspect of a Big Dipper. At the same time, as one travels towards Mae Sariang, the scenery becomes more spectacular and, despite the patches cleared by the hilltribes, there is sufficient lush forest to make the hills truly stunning.

At KM 55 the village of **Ban Kong Loi** lies over to the left. This was once a Karen settlement but in recent years it has been largely incorporated into mainstream society and the villagers no longer wear their traditional dress for daily wear. Nevertheless, the village, clinging to the hillside, is attractive with its neat wooden houses fronted by small terraced rice fields.

There is a sharp hairpin bend after KM 73 from where H 108 proceeds in a series of spectacular switchbacks. The road and the natural scenery remain the most exciting aspect of the journey although at KM 81 there is a good view to the left across the valley to a typical Karen village, characterised by its thatched roofs in the traditional style of eaves sloping not only front and back but also at the sides of the houses.

Mae Sariang. After the switchbacks and stunning scenery, H 108 gradually descends into the valley of the Yuam river to reach Mae Sariang, 104km from Hot.

Just before reaching the town the highway skirts around to the right while a secondary road leads straight on into the town centre.

Mae Sariang, comprising mostly two-storeyed wooden shophouses, was virtually cut off from the outside world until the opening of H 108 in 1965. Accordingly, despite some inevitable changes, it still possesses an individual character that is perhaps its main attraction. Apart from one or two shops selling Karen handicrafts and the early morning market — worth a half hour's stroll — the only real interest for the traveller are two Burmese-style temples located directly across the road from the Mitaree Hotel in the town centre. (It was not possible to ascertain the name of this street; even the reception clerk in the hotel did not know it!)

Wat Utthayarom (Jong Sung), built in 1896, and the more impressive **Wat Sri Boonruang**, dating from 1939, are fascinating for their typical Burmese-style architecture that typifies many of the religious buildings in the region. This influence is marked by many-tiered roofs of corrugated iron saved from being ugly by intricate filigree work in metal or wood on eaves, gable ends and portico surrounds.

To the right inside the main gate to the compound is Wat Utthayarom along with three **chedis** the last of which is distinguished by its nine spires. Beyond is Wat Sri Boonruang — the more decorative of the two — while nearby is the monks, quarters which for the visitor holds the greatest interest. It takes the typical form of a long wooden building raised on stilts and painted yellow and topped with the inevitable corrugated iron roof. The interior is again exemplary of the Burmese style, being somewhat garishly decorated with a mix of paintings depicting scenes from the lives of the Buddha along with a motley selection of photographs of members of the Thai Royal Family and various distinguished monks of the past. Furnishings include the ubiquitous standing clock, cabinets holding religious texts and an altar with three Buddha images. All combine to create a peaceful homelike atmosphere and, should you speak Thai or be accompanied by a Thai friend, it is pleasant to while away a few minutes in conversation with the abbot over a glass of cold tea.

From Mae Sariang H 108 turns northward towards Mae Hong Son. Three kilometres beyond the town, the road passes the **Huaychompu Teak Arboretum** on the right and for the next few kilometres it continues broad, rising only gently. This can lull you into a false sense of security as it is in no way indicative of the path that lies ahead.

Ban Mae Tia. A dirt track on the left 15km from Mae Sariang leads directly into the Karen village of Ban Mae Tia. This is a largish permanent settlement with its own rice fields and the pathways between the houses are wide enough for a car to drive around, permitting a comfortable way of getting a quick insight into village life — just beware of mother pigs and their offspring meandering across your path; damage to these valuable assets would not be appreciated.

Just before KM 132 (distance from Hot not Mae Sariang) there is a small white **chedi** on the hill to the right while to the left is a fine view across a valley of patchwork rice fields to the tranquil village of **Ban Mae La Noi.** Beyond the village the continuation of the road can be seen as it loops around the valley before climbing into the hills again.

There is generally very little traffic along the way which is fortunate since some 54km from Mae Sariang H 108 narrows to a barely two-car width and is made more difficult by rising and falling steeply through a series of 'S' bends. It can be a trifle embarrassing should the public bus be encountered coming in the opposite direction!

These 'S' bends mark the worst stretch but until just before Mae Hong Son the road remains narrow, weaving its way up, down and around the hills, sometimes seeming to soar above the lush green vegetation and at other times sinking, to be hemmed in on both sides by dense jungle.

This is teak country and at any time other than during the hot season (March to June) loggers and elephants can often be seen at work hauling timber from the forest to roadside collection points. It is also good to stop occasionally just to take in the silence of the forest; complete peace broken only by the cry of birds and the chirping of crickets.

The forested mountain scenery gives way only now and then to small, tucked-away cultivated valleys although at **Amphoe Khun Yuam** (67km from Ban Mae La Noi) the landscape does open up briefly to reveal the lush fertile upper valley of the Yuam river. The sizeable settlement itself is inhabited by a mixture of Thai Yais (Shans) and Lawa tribespeople.

Beyond the valley H 108 continues its journey through the hills until 18km before reaching Mae Hong Son (55km after Khun Yuam) where it begins to descend. At this spot there is a superb view to the right, down into the steep V-shaped valley of the Cha river, a tributary of the Pai river. From here H 108 enters the valley of the Pai in which Mae Hong Son is located.

Mae Hong Son. On the outskirts of the town H 108 curves right to end as Mae Hong Son's main street while H 1095 forks left, skirts the town and after a few kilometres deteriorates into a rough, unsurfaced road which turns southeast to pass through the town of Pai and eventually join H 107.

Wat Kham Kho,
Mae Hong Son

67

Surrounded by forested and often mist-shrouded mountains, Mae Hong Son is a sleepy little settlement made up mostly of two-storeyed wooden shophouses although it does have two reasonable modern hotels — the **Mitrniyom**, on the left just before the town centre, and the **Mae Tee** on the right in the heart of the town.

Mae Hong Son as a permanent settlement did not exist until the mid-19th century but long before that the area was frequented by Shans from Burma, who made seasonal migrations to work the forests, and by various groups of hilltribes — notably Lisu, Lawa, Meo and Karen. This ethnic mix survives today and the province of which Mae Hong Son town is the capital has a population of only 2% ethnic Thais; the remainder being made up of 50% Shans (Thai Yai) and 48% hilltribe people. The latter remain mostly in their own close-knit villages in the hills although individuals are frequently seen in town, especially at the morning market.

Statue of Buddha, Wat Hua Wiang, Mae Hong Son

The settlement of the area began in 1831 when the ruler of Chiang Mai, finding himself somewhat short of those valuable beasts, elephants, sent out an expedition under Chao Kaew-Muang to hunt down and train pachyderms for work. At first a base was established at Ban Pon Mu (now called Ban Pang Mu) on the banks of the Pai river, but later a large number of elephants were caught a few kilometres farther south and Chao Kaew-Muang brought together a number of Shans to build a corral on the site of what was to become Mae Hong Son. The camp for elephants turned into a village and gradually more and more Shans began to make a permanent home in the place they had previously visited only seasonally.

Such was the rapid development of Mae Hong Son and so great the influx of Shans that, in 1874, the then ruler of Chiang Mai deemed it wise to constitute the place as a city and appointed its first full-time ruler, Phraya Singhanatdraja. Three more rulers were to follow him until, in 1893, the area was established as a province under Thailand's Ministry of the Interior with Mae Hong Son as the provincial capital.

Today, the principal attraction of Mae Hong Son is its Shangri-la type setting and its air of tranquillity. Nothing much happens there and that is its charm; you can wander about at peace and feel pleasantly cut off from the rest of the world. The town is close to the Burmese border and while no official crossing exists, a certain amount of smuggling does take place and this adds a tinge of secrecy to the atmosphere of the town.

Yet a sense of escape is not all that Mae Hong Son has to offer (it is ironic, though, to ponder that a sense of escape is the very reverse of what earlier, unwilling visitors must have felt). To see the town at its liveliest — and it is the only time it is lively — a visit to the morning market behind the Mae Tee Hotel is a must. Here, between 6 and 8 a.m., there is a hive of activity around stalls laden with all kinds of fruit, vegetables, spices, meats, clothes and household goods. And where the stalls finish, produce is laid out on leaves along the roadside. Hilltribe people rub shoulders with townfolk and there is a kaleidoscope of faces ranging from the smiles of pretty young girls to the wizened look of old women contentedly puffing away on fat, hand-rolled cheroots.

Besides the morning market, Mae Hong Son's other attraction is a handful of typical Burmese-style temples. The best starting point for a tour of these is **Doi Kong Mu**, the 424m high hill that dominates the town.

To reach Doi Kong Mu, go to the outskirts of town and turn right on to H 1095 and then, after 200m, a turning on the left leads up to the summit — a good paved road all the way. It is 2.4km to the top and about halfway the road forks; straight on leads to the radio relay station while the right-hand fork goes to the two **chedis** on the crest of the hill.

These two **chedis** of **Wat Phrathat Doi Kong Mu**, built in 1860 and 1874 respectively, and the several surrounding images are fascinating in themselves but the real reward of Doi Kong Mu is the magnificent view it affords of the town, the fertile valley and the surrounding green mountains. The enchantment of the panorama is heightened by the tinkling of the bells atop the **chedis** which at night are lit up like Christmas trees, making the scene even more magical. (Loy Krathong festival — end-Oct/early-Nov — is celebrated in an unusual way here with **krathongs**, instead of being floated on rivers and ponds, attached to balloons and sent floating skyward from the Hilltop.)

At the foot of Doi Kong Mu, on the right of the turning off H 1095, is **Wat Phra Non.** The temple has been rebuilt but it does house two large concrete Buddha statues, one a 12m long reclining image and the other a seated Buddha. With their painted, human-like faces, these are typical of the Burmese style.

Behind Wat Phra Non are two giant stone Burmese lions which guard the entrance to the original pathway up Doi Kong Mu. A few metres farther along is a row of six **chedis** built on a raised platform; all that remains of **Wat Muay Toh.**

Directly across the road from Wat Phra Non is the more interesting **Wat Kham Kho**, built in 1890. The covered walkway from the main gate and the **viharn** are roofed in the inevitable corrugated iron but enlivened by tottering tiers decorated with intricate filigree work on the eaves.

Inside the **viharn** are five main Buddha images, the central one being in the Burmese style while the one on the right is typically Thai with its pointed headdress. Behind these are many important old religious objects including a number of small carved 'Buddha Palaces' containing images. In front of the altar is an 80-year-old, beautifully carved Peacock throne decorated with inlaid coloured glass.

The remainder of the interior is decorated with paintings, photographs and the usual clutter of objects that make these northern temples seem so lovingly inhabited — the raised corner where the abbot sits is delightfully equipped with a telephone and refrigerator.

Close to the morning market in the centre of town is **Wat Hua Wiang**, a temple looking even more dilapidated than is usually the case with the wood and corrugated iron architectural style. Appearances can be deceptive, however, and the **wat** enshrines a fine brass seated Buddha that is a copy of a statue in Mandalay and was cast in Burma before being transported by land and river and assembled in Mae Hong Son.

Two other temples, **Wat Chong Kam** and **Wat Chong Klang**, are picturesquely located in the same compound bordering a small tree-fringed lake on the southern side of town. Of particular interest here is the collection of wooden dolls housed in a small barred room to the right just inside the entrance to the **viharn** of Wat Chong Klang. These 33 statues, the tallest being about 1 m high, represent figures from the story of **Vessantara Jataka** (the Jataka are the previous lives of the Buddha) and were brought to Mae Hong Son from Burma in 1857.

At the other end of the compound beside Wat Chong Kam is a building enshrining the revered statue of **Luang Poh To**, a 5m high concrete sitting Buddha.

Excursions. From Mae Hong Son it is possible to make excursions to **Tham Pla** (Fish Cave), **Pha Sua Waterfall** and, farther afield, the large cave of **Tham Lod**. However, all but the first are difficult to reach by ordinary car and the traveller is best advised to hire a minibus truck in town.

Tham Pla. Leave Mae Hong Son from the north via H 1095 and at KM 17.6 turn left down an unsurfaced track that leads 200m to a parking area. From here a small, narrow suspension bridge (watch your step as the slats are not evenly spaced) crosses a stream on the other side of which a path through an attractive grove leads to Tham Pla (a 5-minute walk). The cave is actually a rock pool at the base of a cliff where a subterranean stream surfaces. The pool contains a number of tame fish (**pla muang** or **pla pluang hin**), the biggest up to a metre long, which rise to the surface to be fed (bags of food can be bought from the park keeper's hut on the right, half way along the path). To the right of the pool an alcove in the rock-face houses a small shrine and the fish below are considered holy and thus protected. The whole area is pretty and peaceful and a few wooden picnic tables are scattered about the grove.

Pha Sua Waterfall. Travel north on H 1095 and just before KM 17, at the bottom of a steep incline, turn sharp left on to a dirt track. After 2km the track crosses a wooden bridge and 300 metres later enters the Thai Yai village of **Mok Cham Pae**. In the village take first left, then right and then the right-hand fork at the end of the hamlet. The rough track now rises and falls sharply giving good views of the surrounding mountains. The parking area for the waterfall is on the right 8.7km beyond the village. (The road continues to rise for another 10km to reach the King's residence of Pang Tong.)

Rough steps cut out of the earth lead down to the waterfall which is smaller than Mae Klang but still impressive. There is a broad ledge over which the water tumbles in half a dozen separate flows although in the rainy season (when unfortunately the track is virtually impassable) the water falls in a continuous curtain.

Tham Lod. The rarely visited cave of Tham Lod lies off H 1095 some 80km from Mae Hong Son. It is difficult to reach since the highway ceases to be surfaced after the first 28km and rapidly deteriorates into a steep, winding, rocky track. The views of the mountains, however, are even more impressive than those seen on the drive from Mae Sariang to Mae Hong Son, and they get better in direct proportion to the deterioration of the road. Especially spectacular panoramas can be seen off to the left (towards Burma) between KM 49 and KM 51.

After KM 52 thick jungle encroaches on both sides of the track, obscuring the view, and eight kilometres farther on, the road passes through a cultivated valley. Just beyond, H 1095 goes through the Lisu village of **Sop Pong** where the tribespeople present a colorful sight with their bright green or blue pantaloons.

Roughly 72km from Mae Hong Son (kilometre markers ran out long ago) there is a small Lisu village on the right while opposite a trail leads off left to Tham Lod. One kilometre down this, a stream has to be forded and only a truck can manage it. Hemmed in by jungle, the track continues 5km beyond the stream and then forks; take the right-hand fork which leads into a Thai Yai village where guides for the cave can be hired (the going rate is around 30 baht for men and 10 baht for boys). Guides are essential as there are no lights in the cave and guides provide torches in the form of bundles of kindling pinewood.

The entrance to the cave is 1km after the village and here there is the house of the Forestry Department park keeper who will also act as a guide if necessary. From the parking area it is a 300m walk — half uphill and half down — to the mouth of the cave. Tham Lod is about 300-400m long and is high and broad with a shallow stream running through it. There is no clear pathway and it is necessary to wade back and forth across the stream to make headway.

Inside the cave, believed to be some 9,000 years old, are some interesting limestone formations and high up in niches near the rear entrance (you have to be a bit of a mountain goat to make the climb up, although there are some bamboo ladders to help) are remains of recently found prehistoric wooden coffins.

Emerging from the rear entrance of the cave it is a 20-minute walk along a jungle trail back to the parking area. A visit to Tham Lod is not easy but it is rewarding, especially for those with a taste for adventure.

Return to Chiang Mai. H 1095 goes from Mae Hong Son to Pai and then continues southeast to join H 107 by Ban Mae Ma-lai from where it is 35km back to Chiang Mai. Buses cover the route but, as mentioned, the road is in extremely poor condition and while it improves somewhat beyond Pai, it is not recommended for ordinary cars. A car can make the journey providing there has been no rain but the driver should be prepared for a trying adventure. The alternative is to retrace one's steps back along H 108.

CHIANG MAI TO FANG

Fang, 152km north of Chiang Mai, was originally
founded by King Mengrai in 1268 although today any
trace of a long history is totally lost in the rough and
tumble of a typical border outpost. Nevertheless, the
comparatively short excursion to Fang and beyond to
Tha Thon holds many of the attractions for which the
North is famous — mountains, caves, waterfalls,
hilltribes and perhaps the most exciting river trip
available in Thailand.

Public buses plying the route depart Chiang Mai
every 30 minutes between 5.40 a.m. and 5.30 p.m. and
take approximately 3½ hours to cover the distance.
The Fang road begins at Chiang Mai's White Elephant
Gate and proceeds north along Chotana Road which,
beyond the city, becomes Highway 107. The route
passes the Thai Celadon factory on the right at KM 6
and continues through the broad, fertile plain of the
Ping river.

Mae Sa. Just after passing through the small
settlement of Amphoe Mae Rim, 14km from Chiang
Mai, a signposted turning off to the left leads to the
local beauty spot of the Mae Sa Valley where, in
addition to picturesque scenery, attractions include the
Mae Sa Waterfall and an elephant training camp.

Along the way are a shrimp farm and restaurant,
1.4km from the turnoff, (artificial ponds stocked with
shrimps and fish; angling possible for a nominal rod
hire fee and 25 baht per kilo of catch) and, 1km
beyond, 'Sai Nam Phung Orchid Nursery' where some
100 species of orchids can be seen (entrance 5 baht).

A narrow side road on the left 4.3km past the
nursery leads to Mae Sa Waterfall and Nature Park. It
is 700m to the parking lot (lined with food stalls) from
where it is a 120m walk to the main waterfall which is
spanned by a small wooden bridge. The water tumbles
over several broad but not steep rocky ledges and,
further up, each a few hundred metres apart, are three

other levels of the waterfall accessible by a pathway. The entire area is scenic and popular for picnics, as witnessed by the profusion of food and drink vendors who manage to set up shop in just about every conceivable nook and cranny.

Back on the main road, 3.3km beyond the turnoff to the waterfall, is **Rintr Village**, a collection of comfortable bungalows and a restaurant with low forested hills as a backdrop. Also on the left, 900m farther on, is the entrance to the **Elephant Camp** (admission 40 baht). Here there is a daily show starting at 9 a.m. with elephants demonstrating their various skills as work animals. More exciting, however, is to take a trek on elephant back through lush jungle. Each animal carries two people and the cost is 250 baht per person for a 2½ hour trek.

The elephant back ride goes to **Mae Sa Valley Resort**, 2.5km by road from the entrance to the Elephant Camp. The resort occupies an extremely

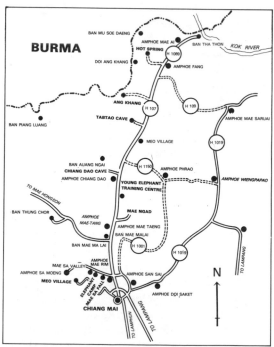

ROUTE MAP:
CHIANG MAI-FANG-THA THON

picturesque, landscaped hillside and in this tranquil setting offers accommodation in well-appointed thatch and bamboo bungalows (single 517 baht and double 572 baht per night). This is an usual type of resort, remote yet easily accessible and, with a good restaurant and full facilities, it is ideal for getting a little peace and relaxation.

Retracing steps back to H 107, the journey north continues through a fertile plain where, in addition to rice, peanuts, vegetables and tobacco are cultivated and the landscape is dotted with the tall, distinctive brick curing houses for the tobacco crop.

Some 38km from Chiang Mai the highway temporarily leaves the valley of the Ping river and enters briefly that of its tributary, the Mae Nam Taeng. This whole area has been extensively developed by the Irrigation Department and owes its fertility to a number of dams and a widespread system of irrigation channels. Two sites in particular, **Mae Taeng Dam** and **Mae Faek**, have been landscaped and are picturesque areas ideal for picnics.

The former lies 7km off to the left on a side road that leaves H 107 1.5km before the town of Mae Taeng (38.2km from Chiang Mai). To reach Mae Faek, on the Ping river, turn right off H 107 just before KM 41 and proceed along a paved road that leads 2.7km to the artificial lake and gardens. A couple of food stalls by the lakeside provide light refreshment in a quiet and tranquil setting.

Irrigation works are on-going in the area and the major project of **Mae Ngad** is currently halfway to completion. A little beyond KM 41 a giant concrete sign announces the turnoff on the right to the construction site 12km away. Here the half-built dam wall can be seen plus the area behind that will eventually become a vast artificial lake providing water transportation as far as Phrao. Construction was started in 1977 and the dam is scheduled to be completed by 1985 at a cost of 960 million baht plus an additional 150 million baht for the generator plant. Principally Mae Ngad is designed to provide an irrigation system although the dam will also produce some 5,000 kwts of electricity.

Young Elephant Training Centre. After KM 49
H 107 makes a sharp downhill curve and the road now
leaves the plain and passes through a gorge cut out by
the Ping river. The scenery changes as the fields give
way to splendid forested hills. A little before KM 56 a
turning on the right leads into the Chiang Dao Young
Elephant Training Centre.

Situated on the banks of the Ping river, this
privately-owned concern trains young elephants in the
basic forest-work skills and every morning at 9.30 a.m.
puts on a show for visitors (admission: adults 40 baht
and children 20 baht). The display begins with the
elephants' routine morning bathe in the river and then
the animals are led to a rough amphitheatre where
they demonstate the various methods of pulling,
dragging and lifting logs, both singly and in pairs. The
show lasts about three quarters of an hour and
afterwards it is possible to take elephant-back rides
around the kraal (10 baht extra).

Hilltribes Development & Welfare Centre. At KM
61.5 a signposted track on the left leads to the
Hilltribes Development & Welfare Centre, Chiang
Mai, a project run by the Department of Public
Welfare and designed to provide hilltribes living on
Doi Chiang Dao and neighbouring mountains with
agricultural assistance, medical care and other
services to help raise living standards.

Lahu Tribespeople

Chiang Dao Cave

The station and nursery for the propagation of a variety of cash crops are located on the hillside at a height of over 1,000m, but the 7km-long track is rough and steep and while passing through superb tropical forests and affording magnificent views, it is passable only by motorbike or truck. Official trucks occasionally pick up passengers at the bottom of the turnoff but as these are unscheduled, the visitor is best advised to hire a minibus truck in Amphoe Chiang Dao which lies a few kilometres farther north along H 107.

Beyond the agricultural station, which is experimenting with the cultivation of tea, coffee and other cash crops, to be introduced as substitutes to the hilltribes' traditional cash crop of opium, are several hilltribe villages. The closest, a Lahu (Muser) settlement, is only 1km away and can be easily visited, but others can only be reached after lengthy treks.

Continuing northwards along H 107, Doi Chiang Dao comes into view on the left, its peak often shrouded in cloud. This is Thailand's third highest mountain with a height of 2,180m (the second highest after Doi Inthanon is Doi Phanhompok, near Fang, which reaches 2,285m). Doi Chiang Dao is a distinctly impressive sight and dominates the landscape for the next stretch of the journey.

79

Chiang Dao Cave. From the Ping river gorge H 107 levels out as it enters the valley of Amphoe Chiang Dao. The town, 72km from Chiang Mai, holds no major attractions although on the northern outskirts on the left is the turning for Chiang Dao Cave.

It is 5km to the foot of the **doi** along a partly paved track that passes through teak plantations, fields and tiny hamlets. Adjacent to the parking area is an old many-spired Burmese-style **chedi** and, adding charm to the scene, a small stream by the stairway leading up to the cave, flows into a pool containing many tame fish **(pla muang)**. An ornamental stone royal barge in the pool and small **chedis** in the rock face above complete the fairyland-like picture.

At the top of the covered stairway is the narrow mouth of the cave (entrance 3 baht) from where a few steps lead down into the first chamber which contains an altar with five seated Buddhas plus an adjacent row of smaller images. More steps lead into another shrine from where a passage continues for about 300m before the lights finish. Halfway along there is on the left a 4m long sleeping Buddha roughly carved out of the limestone while at the end, in a niche up to the right, is a life-size supine statue of Phra Kassapa, one of Lord Buddha's followers.

It is believed that from the point where the lights finish the cave extends for several kilometres but it has yet to be satisfactorily explored, and if anyone has ever proven the legend of a wonderland existing deep within the mountain, he has never returned to tell the tale!

On the slopes of Doi Chiang Dao live a number of hilltribes and it is possible to trek to Lisu, Muser and Karen villages although it is essential to have a guide. Potential trekkers should enquire in the tiny hamlet of **Ban Tham**, 300m back along the track from Chiang Dao Cave for 'Mr. Pom' who offers his services as a guide for 150 baht a day plus 100 baht for porters. An ideal trek, taking in several hilltribe villages and reaching the peak of the mountain, takes 3 days/ 2 nights and the best weather conditions exist from November to January (cool and dry). Trekkers, however, must supply their own camping gear and food, and Mr. Pom requires one week's notice to arrange for porters.

King Naresuan's Monument. Off to the left of H 107 at KM 78.3 lies a **stupa** and reconstructed wooden fort commemorating King Naresuan the Great of Ayutthaya. It was this monarch who repelled a Burmese invasion and slew the Burmese Crown Prince in a duel on elephant-back at Nong Sa Rai, near Suphan Buri, in 1593. He later travelled north to lead an offensive against Burma and won a sizeable amount of territory in the area between Chiang Mai and Fang.

During this offensive King Naresuan rested his army and prepared for battle near the present-day village of Muangngai which is located 4.4km off to the left of H 107 down a partially surfaced track. The **stupa** is 200m to the left by the entrance to the village and behind is the reconstructed wooden stockade comprising a 30m square fenced compound with fortified corner towers and a central keep. The site is picturesquely located in the shadow of Doi Chiang Dao and despite the proximity of the village and the presence of the memorial stupa, everything appears very much as it must have done in Naresuan's time.

Continuing north H 107 leaves the Ping river valley and enters a hilly watershed area. H 1150 branches off to the right by KM 83 and goes to Phrao 32km away. This secondary road is unsurfaced and there is little to recommend a sidetrip although Phrao is famous for a resident monk, Luang Pu Whaen Su Chinno, who is popularly believed to have special powers in blessing amulets.

The scenery through the watershed area is punctuated by some quite spectacular rock outcrops, especially stunning between KM 89 and KM 94. Just beyond, at KM 95 a small hamlet on the right of H 107 marks one of the agricultural sites of the Royal Northern Project where farmers are experimenting with the cultivation of temperate vegetables as potential cash crops.

At the far end of the village a muddy track (impassable in the rainy season) forks left 900m to **Huay Luk Waterfall** which, in truth, is hardly more than a stream passing down the hillside.

A little before KM 96 the Meo village of Huay Luk spans both sides of H 107. It is a sizeable settlement consisting of huts crudely constructed of unseasoned teak which the tribespeople have illegally cut; evidence of further wastage of this valuable wood can be seen in trees cut around the base to induce an untimely death. The women and children here still dress in their traditional costumes although the men, as is becoming increasingly the case, tend to favour the clothes of the ordinary Thai farmer.

From Huay Luk H 107 rises steeply and the landscape of sheer rock formations is reminiscent of the humped limestone mountains of Guilin in China. The climb continues beyond the Muser village of **Ban Hua Toa** at KM 103.5 until KM 109 where the highway begins its long descent into the broad Fang plain.

Tubtao Caves. Three kilometres (not two as the signpost indicates) down a laterite track off to the left by KM 117.8 are Tubtao Caves — and, along the way, fine views of Doi Chiang Dao. Here, in a tranquil leafy glade, is a small wooden hut inhabited by a solitary monk and behind, at the foot of the cliff, are two staircases leading up respectively to 'Light Cave' **(Tham Pha Khaw)** on the right and 'Dark Cave' **(Tham Pan Jeak)** on the left.

Should you speak Thai or be accompanied by a Thai friend, it is pleasant to stop and talk to the monk before climbing up to the caves. He will give you their history while you sit and take in the atmosphere of what seems to be one of the most perfect spots for meditation.

'Light Cave,' so named because it is illuminated by a hole in the roof, is a largish vault, 10 steps down from the entrance. On one side is a giant seated Buddha reaching almost to the roof while on the other side is an open-sided shrine containing a 10-metre brick and cement image of the reclining Buddha surrounded by kneeling statues of devotees paying homage.

'Dark Cave' has a main chamber at the bottom of a flight of 20 steps down from the entrance where there are four seated Buddhas placed adjacent to a curious limestone formation. From here one needs a torch to go and farther; there is said to be a 1,000-year-old

chedi 1.5km into the cave, but this is rarely visited for obvious reasons.

According to legend the caves were formed when one of Lord Buddha's first followers came to the site where he achieved enlightenment just before he died. On his death, angels came to cremate him and the subsequent fire burnt holes in the cliff before a **naga** came along with water to extinguish the flames. Hence the name of the caves which means 'ashes'. The large statue in 'Light Cave' is believed to be 1,000 years old but this is probably an exaggeration. Nevertheless the caves are fascintaing and the location is picturesque and one of great serenity.

Beyond the turnoff for Tubtao H 107 enters the Fang plain and the road flattens out for the remaining 32km to the district centre. On the left by KM 137 is a secondary road that goes 26km to **Ang Khang** agricultural station. This is one of the main experimental nurseries belonging to the Royal Northern Project which is pioneering the propagation of flowers, temperate vegetables and fruits such as peaches, strawberries and pears that are intended as alternative cash crops for the hilltribes whose livelihood until now has been dependent on the growing of opium. It is a very pretty area but unfortunately the track to Ang Khang is too steep and rocky for an ordinary car and a visit is best made by hiring a minibus truck in Fang.

Fang. By KM 151, H 107 becomes once more Chotana Road, this time as the main street of Fang, a small undistinguished district centre close to the Burmese border and comprising mostly two-storeyed wooden shophouses. Back in the 1950s there were high hopes of prosperity when oil was discovered close by, but the reserves did not live up to expectations and the promised boom never came. Today, there is still a small refinery at Mai Sun by KM 141 and about 2km off to the left a few old-style 'donkey' pumps can be seen nodding away. In all there are some 20 wells in use but production is no more than 600 barrels of oil a day — just enough for local consumption.

Fang's only other claim to fame is the especially delicious honey produced by the numerous bees in the area. This is the legitimate side of the coin, on the nefarious side Fang, being close to Burma and deep within the famous (or infamous) 'Golden Triangle,' is inevitably part of the opium smuggling pipeline. This trade is obviously clandestine but the town does possess an air of conspiracy if not lawlessness.

The surrounding border district is occupied by various, and often conflicting, rebel factions — remnants of Chiang Kai-shek's Kuomintang Chinese troops, Karen liberation armies, communist insurgents and, most notably, the Shan United Army commanded by notorious opium warlord Khun Sa. Political causes, however, take second place to gaining a slice of the opium traffic.

Although fighting does sometimes take place between rebel factions, it is usually limited to the hills on the Burmese side of the border. Occasionally Thai troops will conduct 'clean-up' swoops along the border area. Basically Fang is secure with the Thai Border Patrol Police having a good grip on the situation but travellers should be wary about trekking in remote areas. Treks are organized by some of the small hotels in the town and there are some good hilltribe villages to be visited, but check on the security situation before setting out — some tourists in the past have been robbed and worse. This is a sensitive area and there are good reasons why remote spots remain remote.

The principal attractions of a visit to Fang — the Horticultural Station and Hot Springs and boat trips on the Kok river — are not in the town itself and the place, with a handful of small hotels, serves mostly as a base. Fang does, however, afford the simple pleasure of people-watching. Being a border outpost, it bustles in its own small way and the passersby are made more colourful and varied by the diverse hilltribe people in from the surrounding countryside on shopping expeditions. A good vantage point for taking in the scene is the Ku Charoen Chai restaurant (the best eating place in town) at 136 Chotana Road, just across from the market.

Horticultural Station & Hot Springs. By KM 151 at the entrance to Fang a signposted turnoff on the left leads to Fang Horticultural Experimental Station. After

400m down this side road turn left on to a laterite track and then right after 1.6km from where it is a further 4.6km to the Station. Here such crops as coffee, apples, peaches and various vegetables are propagated to provide plants for the neighbouring villages.

Another 2.6km beyond the horticultural station are the **Baw Nam Rawn** sulphur springs. Water bubbles out of the ground at near boiling point in many places scattered throughout a rocky field while the air is permeated with the smell of sulphur. At present it is a pleasant location with forested hills providing a scenic backdrop but this may change since the government is planning to build a power station to tap the resources of the hot springs.

Tha Thon. The small settlement of Tha Thon, on the banks of the Kok river, lies 24km north of Fang along H H 1089 (in reality an extension of H 107). It is a pretty drive and the beauty of the national scenery in this area becomes even more evident from the river excursions available from Tha Thon.

As one enters the hamlet, just before the bridge spanning the river, **Wat Tha Thon** stands on the hillside to the left while on the right a short track leads

Kok River

down the river bank to the boathouse. From this landing stage longtail boats leave daily at 12.30 p.m. for the 4-5 hour trip downstream to Chiang Rai. The one-way fare is 160 baht per person or, alternatively, travellers can hire their own boat, taking up to eight passengers, for 1,600 baht. (A word of warning: occasionally boats have been held up and robbed. Such incidents are now rare due to the activities of the Border Patrol Police and the danger is minimal these days but not non-existent.)

For the adventurous the trip downriver to Chiang Rai can be accomplished by bamboo raft in three days/two nights. Complete with a crude cabin and taking up to six passengers, these rafts are custom built and cost 2,200 baht each — this price includes the construction costs, services of a boatman for the journey plus a supply of blankets, mats and a stove; food is extra. Rafts can be ordered by asking at the boathouse and 10-days notice should be given. The best time of the year for making the trip is between October and January.

Whether by longtail boat or by raft, the journey down the Kok river to Chiang Rai is one of the very best river excursions possible in Thailand. Not only is the natural scenery exceptionally beautiful but also the journey passes over a number of rapids (not 'white water' but fun nevertheless), passes by several hilltribe villages (Muser and Karen), and other attractions such as **Tham Phra** cave some 15 minutes upstream from Chiang Rai. The regular daily boat makes only one stop at the passport check of Mae Salak, one hour from Tha Thon, and the traveller is therefore better off taking his own boat or raft which will stop at all places of interest.

For the traveller without time or inclination to make the full trip to Chiang Rai, short boat excursions can be made, the most popular of which visits **Ban Mai Mork Charm**, one and a half hours from Tha Thon by longtail boat, where Akha, Lahu and Lisu hilltribes can be seen. It is also possible to stay overnight in this village in hilltribe houses at a cost of 15-20 baht per person per night.

Basic accommodation is available in Tha Thon at the **Chankasem Bungalow & Restaurant** which is located at the end of the short track along the river bank. Overnight rates are between 60 and 100 baht.

The Kok river trip is the ideal way to reach Chiang Rai but the traveller with his own transport is best advised to retrace steps back along H 107 to Chiang Mai and take the new road (H 1019) back up to Chiang Rai. This may seem an unnecessarily roundabout route since Chiang Rai is only about 70km east of Fang as the crow flies. However, while H 109 does cut across from H 107 south of Fang to join H 1019 at Mae Suai, it is an unsurfaced road and in poor condition. Thus it is not only quicker but also more comfortable to return to Chiang Mai before heading north again.

CHIANG MAI TO CHIANG RAI AND THE GOLDEN TRIANGLE

The journey northeast to Chiang Rai and beyond to the so-called 'Golden Triangle' is perhaps the most popular excursion from Chiang Mai. This region is the most northerly part of Thailand and for many travellers it epitomizes the entire North. It has all the ingredients — mountain scenery, hilltribes, temples, work elephants etc. — but more especially it has the 'Golden Triangle.'

The 'Golden Triangle' is the area that produces three-quarters of the world's supply of opium. The name was coined by the press and repeated usage in the media and sensational fiction has given it an absurd popularity. The 'triangle' is roughly an equilateral one with its base running through Chiang Mai, or just below, into Burma in the west and Laos in the east. The sides take in large chunks of Burmese

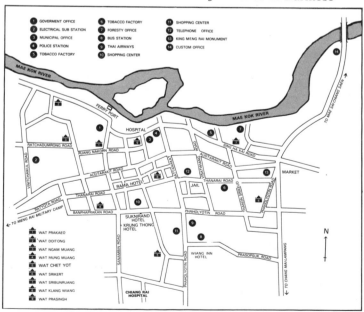

CITY MAP OF CHIANG RAI

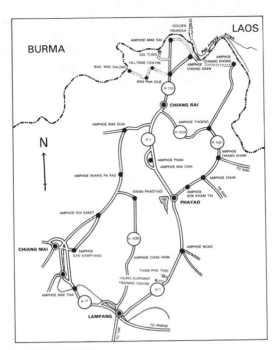

ROUTE MAP:
CHIANG MAI-CHIANG RAI-PHAYAO-LAMPANG

and Laotian territory and the apex is a little north of where the boundaries of the three countries meet. Although Chiang Rai province is in the very heart of the opium producing area, the spot actually designated the Golden Triangle' in the province is the place near Chiang Saen where Thailand, Burma and Laos meet. This, far from swarming with fierce opium warlords, is a tranquil and picturesque spot.

The opium poppy can be seen growing in some places in the hills north of Chiang Rai (the plants are only obvious to the uninitiated when they flower in December/January), but Royal and Government projects are increasingly making headway in introducing alternative cash crops to the farmers, the hilltribes. The name 'Golden Triangle' may conjure up images of wily opium warlords and secret jungle trails, but the far north has in reality many more genuine attractions and has no need to rely on a dubious reputation for its allure.

Chiang Rai is easily reached by car, bus or plane. Since the opening of the new road (H 1019) a few years ago, the land journey takes only 3½ hours from Chiang Mai as opposed to the 5-6 hours by the old route via Lampang and Highway 1. Flying time is 40 minutes. Buses leave the northern capital every 30 minutes from 6 a.m. to 5.30 p.m. and the two daily Thai Airways flights depart at 9.15 a.m. and 1.05 p.m. respectively.

By car the journey to Chiang Rai begins at Ta Pae Gate. To reach H 1019, drive east across Nawarat Bridge after which turn left and follow the river bank for 900m, turn right at the traffic lights down Kaeo Nawarat Road and at the second set of lights, after 1km, the Chiang Rai highway lies straight on (signposted Mae Kachan 79km).

Just after KM 14 the highway forks; H 1019 branches to the left while to the right leads to Doi Saket (see page 41). At first paddy fields border the road and the scenery is flat but some 21km from Chiang Mai the landscape becomes hilly and the fields give way to trees which in April and May are especially attractive as wild orchids bloom among their branches.

Close to KM 41 Doi Saket Elephant Camp lies off to the right. It is one of the smaller training schools in the North but it does put on a show in the early morning which is worth seeing if the traveller has not had a chance to visit any of the larger, better known elephant camps.

Four kilometres farther on, the road passes a Karen village on the left and the scenery is now extremely attractive with hills, forests and the occasional sleepy village. The peak of the hills is reached at **Doi Nang Kaew** (KM 53) and 1km beyond, the driver should be wary of a sharp curve (signposted) as H 1019 begins to descend.

At KM 65 there is a rest area by the right side of the road with a food stall set up by a small stream and a few hot springs. The terrain is now flatter although the surrounding countryside of trees and rolling hills in the background is still most pleasant.

The small settlement of **Ban Mae Kachan** (the rest stop for the Chiang Mai-Chiang Rai bus) is by KM 77 and 16km farther on is the small town of **Wiang Pa Pao**, the halfway point. Neither place has much of interest although they do provide refreshment. Just before Wiang Pa Pao a laterite road (H 1150) branches left to pass through Phrao and later join the Fang road (H107).

Some 8km beyond Wiang Pa Pao H 1019 rises into the hills again for about 7km before descending into a broad fertile valley. All of this area is noted for its delicious sweetcorn which can be bought, steamed or grilled, from the several roadside stalls encountered along the way.

A little way beyond **Mae Suai** (KM 132) H 109 (unsurfaced) heads off left to join H 107 south of Fang. The scenery is briefly of hills again until the highway passes the Mae Nam Lao and, 20km later, joins H 1 which continues north across a broad plain for the remaining 23km to Chiang Rai.

The small pottery village of **Ban Pong Sali** is passed on the left after 12.7km and at the junction 6.6km farther on (near KM 825 — distance from Bangkok) right (H 1020) leads 137km to Chiang Khong; left enters Chiang Rai via Phaholyothin Road and straight on skirts around the city.

Chiang Rai. This provincial capital, located on the banks of the Kok river and comprising mostly two-storeyed concrete shophouses, is clean, quiet and pleasant. A good deal of building has taken place in recent years but there is, nevertheless, a decided lack of activity. One gets the impression that everything has been prepared for the coming of a boom similar to that which has hit Chiang Mai, but its imminent arrival is in no way indicated and the pace of life remains leisurely.

The city was founded in 1262 by King Mengrai who was at that time beginning the southerly expansion of his territory from his former power centre at Chiang Saen. If legend is to be believed, the site was taken to be auspicious since it was here that one of Mengrai's favourite elephants was recaptured after it had run away.

Such a long history, however, is not readily evident in the Chiang Rai of today and the principal attractions are limited to a handful of temples.

Wat Phra Singh, on Singhakai Road near the Town Hall, formerly housed the important image of **Phra Buddha Si Hing** which is now enshrined in the temple of the same name in Chiang Mai. A copy of the statue is today to be seen in the Chiang Rai temple.

Wat Phra Kaeo, near Wat Phra Singh on Trirat Road, has a nicely decorated **bot** and **viharn** but is primarily noted for its **chedi** where, it is said, the famous Emerald Buddha (now in Wat Phra Kaeo in Bangkok) was discovered in 1436 during the reign of King Sam Fang Kaen of Chiang Mai. Lightning is supposed to have damaged the **chedi** thus exposing the statue which was at that time disguised with a plaster covering. Some time later the plaster cracked revealing the true value of the image. (It is in fact made of green jasper and not emerald.)

Wat Ngam Muang, sited on a hill west of Wat Phra Kaeo and reached by a short flight of **naga**-flanked stairs, possesses an ancient brick **chedi** which is the reliquary for the remains of King Mengrai. It was built by his son, Chao Khun Kram, in 1318.

Wat Doi Tong, on a hill north of Wat Ngam Muang, comprises a **bot** and **chedi** but, more significantly, also commands a fine view out over the Kok river and surroundings. It is believed that it was from this vantage point that King Mengrai first surveyed the site that was to become Chiang Rai. The **chedi** has been restored several times, lastly in 1945 by a Burmese monk which accounts for its Burmese style of architecture.

Wat Klang Wiang, on Rattanakhet Road, probably built in the early Rattanakosin era, enshrines a 4-metre high Chiang Saen-style Buddha.

Wat Chet Yot, a little to the west of the Wiang Inn Hotel, derives its name from its **chedi** with seven **(chet)** spires that was copied from the temple of the same name in Chiang Mai.

Apart from these temples, the only other monument of interest is the statue of King Mengrai which stands in a park on the eastern edge of the city.

While Chiang Rai is certainly worth at least a half-day's exploration, it is more especially the ideal centre from which to make excursions to the far north. It has a number of hotels in all price ranges from deluxe to guesthouse as well as several good restaurants. Highly recommended is the restaurant on the banks of the Kok river close to the boat landing stage — the food is good and the setting restful and picturesque.

Trekking

For travellers without their own transport and wishing to travel further afield than the buses to Mae Sai and Chiang Saen permit, trekking tours to hilltribe villages and other places of interest are organized by three of the town's guesthouses. Prices range from 350 baht for a 2-day trek to 850 baht for seven days. Arrangements can be made at the following: Pongpun Guesthouse on Ngam Muang Road; Chiang Rai Guesthouse, Srikeud Road and Pron Guesthouse on Rattanakhet Road.

To Mae Sai and Chiang Saen

Mae Sai, Thailand's most northerly town, lies at the end of H 110 (extension of H 1). From Chiang Rai centre turn left by the statue of King Mengrai on to the main highway, following the signpost indicating Mae Chan, 28km away. Just beyond the city the road crosses the Kok river and passes through a landscape of fields and low-lying hills in the distance.

Mae Chan. A loop road off to the left 26.9km from Chiang Rai leads into the centre of Mae Chan, a small trading town that supplies household goods to the hilltribes that live in the surrounding area. This small but prosperous-looking settlement is also known for the excellent quality of its lychees.

Rejoining H 110, 100m beyond Mae Chan the road forks; to the left is Mae Sai 32km away while the right-hand fork leads 31km to Chiang Saen. Take the Mae Sai road and after 2.3m (by KM 860 — distance from Bangkok) turn left on to H 1130 which is signposted in English 'Hilltribe Development and Welfare Centre 12km, Doi Mae Salong (Ban Santikhiri) 36m.' H 1130 is surfaced only for the first 3.7km after which it becomes laterite.

Hilltribe Centre. For the first part of the journey H 1130 runs through a lush fertile valley before climbing into the gently undulating hills. The scenery is exceptionally attractive and becomes more so the farther one progresses.

The Thai village of **Mae Salong Nai** is reached after 6.2km from the turnoff and 5.1km beyond that is the settlement of **Ban Pa Miang**. Less than a kilometre from the village a track on the right leads up to the Hilltribe Centre managed by the Department of Public Welfare.

The Centre, with a staff of 200, provides hilltribe villagers living in the area with assistance in occupational and social development, home industries and the propagation of cash crops such as coffee, lychees, maize, sesame and soya beans.

The number of tribespeople in Chiang Rai and Phayao provinces totals more than 51,300 of which Yao and Akha are the most numerous while Meo, Lisu and Muser are also well represented. From talking with the Centre personnel the traveller can gain much valuable information regarding the hilltribes and the work being carried out by the Government to help raise their standard of living. The Centre also has a small selection of handicrafts for sale.

En Route to Doi Mae Salong

Wat Phrathat, Doi Thung

Beyond the Hilltribe Centre H 1130 twists and turns as it climbs further into the hills. The Yao village of **Ban Pha Dua** is located on the left 5.8km from the Centre. This is a sizeable settlement of some 500 inhabitants and 59 houses constructed on the hillside. Pigs, dogs and chickens roam freely and a farmyard-like odour is witness to the authenticity of the village. Authentic though it is, women and children decked out in full tribal regalia are well versed in the art of hawking embroidered bags and other handicrafts as soon as a visitor shows his face.

From Ban Pha Dua the road snakes around up the hill permitting after a few hundred metres a superb vista back down over the village, the lower hills and the plain stetching far out into the distance. The views get better and better further up the mountain while the road gets progressively worse.

Another hilltribe village, **Ban Iko Sam Yaek**, belonging to the Akha tribe lies 5.9km farther along the road on the right. A turning here goes 13km to **Ban Thoed Thai (Hin Taek)** where notorious opium warlord Khun Sa formerly maintained a house.

Mae Salong. The journey to Mae Salong, a Chine Haw (Kuomintang Chinese) settlement at the summit of the mountain, continues up between hillsides that are mostly under cultivation, in places with opium poppy. Just over nine kilometres from Ban Iko Sam Yaek is the tiny hamlet of **Wang Klang** immediately beyond which the road rises very steeply through a 100m stretch before continuing more gently the remaining 3.2km up to Mae Salong.

Settled more than 20 years ago in a beautiful, isolated spot, Mae Salong is a comparatively large village of bamboo-sided, corrugated iron-roofed houses perched on the slopes at the summit of Doi Mae Salong. The villagers support themselves by the cultivation of coffee, tea and maize and some surprising trade judging by the shops which display Thai, Chinese, Burmese and Western products. In such a remote place it is strange to see on the shelves 'Marlboros' rubbing shoulders with Burmese-made cigarettes.

But then, Mae Salong is indeed a remarkable village. Set high amid magnificent mountain scenery, it is more than just quiet and tranquil; it is seemingly a world unto itself, cut off from anywhere else and possessing an air of complete autonomy. Pack horses add charm to the place which welcomes the traveller — there is even a small, wooden 10-room hotel (50 baht a night) — yet keeps itself to itself.

Mae Salong may not be as colourful as a typical hilltribe village (a few tribespeople do live nearby, however) but it is nevertheless well worth visiting for both its stunning location and its mysterious atmosphere.

Doi Thung. After retracing one's steps back to H 110, another mountain, Doi Thung, lies away to the left 5.6km beyond **Ban Mae Kham** near KM 871. The turnoff (H 1149) is signposted in English and the road is surfaced although narrow and steep in places. As with the trip to Doi Mae Salong, the journey up Doi Thung affords some splendid views.

The first few villages encountered along the way are Thai Yai (Shan) but 6.8km from the turnoff there is the Akha settlement of **Ban Pa Kha**, an authentic tribal settlement yet boasting the 'Paca Guesthouse' which offers basic accommodation (no food) in 10 primitive huts for 20 baht a night. Another three Akha villages can be seen in the next 6-7km, each distinguished by the typical Akha custom of building their huts with the roofs sweeping close to the ground so that there are hardly any walls.

A Muser village is located on the left 7.7kms beyond Ban Pa Kha after which the road peters out and a dirt track covers the remaining 3.3km to the top of the **doi**. From here a short, rough, muddy path leads down to the entrance of **Wat Phra That Doi Thung** which nestles just below the summit nearly 2,000m above sea level.

The word **thung** means 'flag', and the mountain derives its name from the fact that, according to the chronicles, King Achutaraj of the Singhanawat dynasty of Chiang Saen ordered a giant flag to be flown from the mountain peak to mark the sight of two **chedis** he had built to enshrine relics of Lord Buddha in 911.

A small **viharn** and **bot** were much later built next to the **chedis** which were restored in 1973. The temple is important enough to attract an annual pilgrimage but the real reward of a visit is the fantastic view of the surrounding mountains, the valley far below and the plain beyond encompassing vast expanses of Thai and Burmese territory.

Mae Sai. Returning to H 110, Mae Sai is 19km away to the north. Midway to the town, **Khunnam Nang Non**, or 'Sleeping Lady Mountain,' can be seen off to the left. This extended mountain range derives its name from the fact that its outline roughly resembles that of a woman sleeping on her back — the profile of the face is fairly recognizable but the rest of the body is anatomically a little strange.

Mae Sai, 891km from Bangkok, is as far north as Thailand goes. The town is on the banks of the river of the same name which forms the border with Burma. A bridge provides a crossing although it is open only to Thais and Burmese (foreigners are not permitted to enter Burma by land) and the one-horse town owes its prosperity to border trade and to the popularity of the village on the Burmese side, **Tha Kee Lek**, with Thais who enjoy a visit to buy souvenirs, herbs, various Chinese products and other items not readily available in Thailand.

There are three small hotels should one want to overnight at Mae Sai but apart from the usual fascination generated by a border town, there is little to detain the visitor except **Wat Phra That Doi Wao**. The temple is approached by a lane off to the left of Phaholyothin Road (the main street and continuation of H 110) just before the Top North Hotel a few hundred metres from the river. A flight of 207 stairs with a **naga** balustrade leads to the top of the small hill where the **Wat** is located.

Dominating the small compound is a white **chedi** with Buddha images in niches on the four sides and green stone scorpions **(wao)** at the corners of the base. It was originally built in the reign of King Ong Wao of Chiang Saen to hold a hair of Lord Buddha but was completely reconstructed in 1953. The location of the temple, however, is rather more remarkable and affords fine views of the town, the river and Burma beyond.

Chiang Saen. The ancient town of Chiang Saen lies 38km southeast of Mae Sai and the two places are linked by a dirt road but as this is generally impassable by car, it is safer and quicker to take the main road back to the Chiang Saen turnoff (H 1016) just north of Mae Chan.

Chiang Saen is far more interesting and more attractive than Mae Sai. A once powerful, fortified city, its former importance is indicated by the Fine Arts Department's list of 75 ruined monuments outside the walls and 66 inside. Although much of the old fortifications remain intact and more restoration work is being carried out, the ruins of Chiang Saen are not as grand nor as extensive as those of, say, Sukhothai or Si Satchanalai. But, on the other hand, Chiang Saen is still a living town and what monuments there are harmonize perfectly with today's image of a tranquil district centre and market town. The charm is further enhanced by a picturesque location on the banks of the Mekong river.

It is generally accepted among historians that Chiang Saen was built over the ruins of an earlier settlement in 1328 by Phra Chao Saeon Pu, a grandson of King Mengrai. However, most recent research tends to lay more stress on the suggestion that the earlier town must have had considerable power and influence long before the 14th century.

After the rise of Chiang Mai, Chiang Saen became an associate city ruled over by heirs to the Lannathai throne. This state of affairs existed until 1558 when the

Stucco Head of Demon, Chiang Saen Museum

city and surrounding areas were taken over by the Burmese who remained in occupation until the early 19th century when King Rama I retook and sacked the city. It remained abandoned for 70 years until, during the reign of King Rama V, Chao Inta, one of the sons of the Prince of Lamphun, brought back the remnants of Chiang Saen's descendants and rebuilt the town.

H 1016 approaches Chiang Saen from the west, passes between grass-covered mounds — remains of the old city gate — and then swings right to enter the town centre. Just by the old gateway a track off to the left leads to the ruins of **Wat Pa Sak**. Here is Chiang Saen's oldest **chedi** constructed prior to the founding of the city to enshrine sacred relics. It is a magnificent structure in the form of a stepped pyramid, rising to a pointed spire and with niches that formerly housed Buddha images. Its style displays various influences, most notably that of the early Haripunchai period, and the **chedi** has been restored several times, lastly in 1959. The site was originally planted with a hundred teak trees **(sak)** thus giving rise to the name.

From Wat Pa Sak a track continues north beside the city·walls for about 1km to a hill by the northwest corner of the fortifications on top of which is **Wat Phra That Chom Kitti**. An ancient flight of 350 rough steps lead up to the temple although a car can just make it up the narrow 800m track to the top of the hill, from where there is a fine view over the town, the Mekong river and beyond into Laos.

Of principal interest is the 25m high **chedi**, with a slightly leaning top, constructed on a rectangular base and with niches on the four sides containing stucco Buddhas. It is believed to pre-date the city and to have been built in 940 to house part of the forehead bone of Lord Buddha. It has been restored many times, most recently in 1959.

To the side of the **chedi** is a small **sala** containing two large and several smaller Buddha images all of which are replicas of Chiang Saen style except the large one on the right which is in Phitsanulok style. Just below Wat Phra That Chom Kitti, at the top of the staircase, is the small ruined **chedi** of **Wat Chom Chang**.

Returning back to the city gates, just after H 1016 makes its curve to enter the town the **museum** is located on the right-hand side. It contains a small but representative collection of Chiang Saen-style Buddhas and other objects and as such gives a fair introduction to the influential local art. The museum is open from 8.30 a.m. — 12 noon and from 1 p.m. to 4.30 p.m. Wednesday to Sunday. Entrance is free except on Saturday and Sunday when 2 baht is charged.

Next to the museum is **Wat Chedi Luang** noted for its 58m high, octagonal **chedi** said to have been built in 1390 and a good example of early Chiang Mai art. Part of the walls of the old **bot** next to the **chedi** have been roofed over to house a seated Buddha.

From here H 1016 cuts through the town centre before reaching the banks of the Mekong. Along the way are a number of ruined **chedis**, the most notable of which are **Wat Mung Muang, Wat Phra Buat** and **Wat Lan Thong** on the left, right and left sides of the road respectively.

About 1km from the museum H 1016 comes to a 'T' junction by the river. To the left is the village of **Sob Ruak** 11km away and the spot designated as the 'Golden Triangle'; to the right H 1129 goes the 54km to **Chiang Khong**.

Before heading off in either direction it is worth noting that Chiang Saen's best restaurant, **Sala Thai**, is located on the banks of the Mekong at the junction. The food is good and the setting peaceful with a good view across the river into Laos.

To the 'Golden Triangle.' After turning left at the junction, the **Chiang Saen Guesthouse** is on the left. This is the best place to stay in town and provides basic but comfortable accommodation in 10 rooms (17 beds). (There is also the smaller, 5-room **Poon Suk** hotel on the main street opposite the police station.)

Not only does the Chiang Saen Guesthouse provide accommodation, but also its owner, Mr. Somwong, is a mine of information about places of interest in the area and he can arrange for the hire of minibus trucks and bicycles — he even provides a sketch map for excursions by bicycle.

Next to the guesthouse is **Wat Pha Khao Pan**. The

temple is modern but behind is an old 13m high **chedi** originally constructed by the son of Phraya Lawa Changaraj to house sacred relics.

The road continues to parallel the Mekong and shortly deteriorates into a laterite track (this is the road that leads eventually to Mae Sai). A turning on the left 7.4km beyond Wat Pha Khao Pan goes 6km to an Akha village and a few hundred metres past the junction, a signpost announces the 'Golden Triangle.' For a panoramic view of this famous spot climb up the rough steps on the left just before the sign to **Wat Phra That Pu Khao**. On top of the small hill is an ancient brick image hall at the back of which is a niche containing a 1m high, bronze Chiang Saen Buddha. From the temple there is a magnificent view of the river and the 'Golden Triangle.'

The so-called 'triangle' is where the Ruak river empties into the Mekong thus bringing together the boundaries of Thailand, Burma and Laos — the west bank is Thailand, the narrow promontary between the Ruak and Mekong rivers is Burmese territory and the east bank is Laos. A small, quiet guesthouse, the **Golden Hut**, is situated on the banks of the river and offers basic accommodation in 8 rooms for 30 baht single and 60 baht double.

Chiang Khong. Back at the junction with H 1016 in Chiang Saen, the righthand turning is H 1129 which parallels the Mekong southeast to the town of Chiang Khong. After the first few kilometres the road is unsurfaced and can only be negotiated by minibus truck. There is not much, however, to recommend the journey as apart from the Meo village there is little to see and Chiang Khong has lost its former attraction as a hopping-off point for Laos since that country closed its borders.

The closed-door policy of Laos has also lead to the suspension of the boat service down the Mekong from Chiang Saen to Chiang Khong. This was once a popular trip until some of the Thai boats were seized by the Laotian authorities.

Should the traveller wish to visit Chiang Khong, and there are one or two good Meo and Yao hilltribe villages in the vicinity, the best route is via H 1020 that branches off H 1 at Chiang Rai and heads southeast to Thoeng before swinging northward to Chiang Khong.

From Chiang Khong it is possible to continue travelling on to Nan (see P.119) via H 1020 back south to Thoeng, H 1021 to Chiang Kham, H 1148 to Tha Wang Pha and then H 1080 to Nan. It should be pointed out, however, that this northeastern part of the region has only recently been declared free of communist insurgents — just how free remains to be seen.

While the journey along H 1129 from Chiang Saen to Chiang Khong is not recommended, it is worth travelling the first 4.2km (the road is surfaced this far) to **Wat Phra That Pha Ngao**. The temple lies off to the right of the road and is approached via a reconstructed brick gateway topped with a chedi-like structure. The partially ruined **bot** is currently being reconstructed and contains a fine old Buddha image that was discovered buried in the ground in 1976 and amounted to a major archaeological find. Behind this is a large brick and plaster bust which is all that remains of the temple's main statue.

Behind the **bot** is a **chedi** strangely built atop a naturally rounded rock, and in the compound to the left is a small menagerie of caged black bears and monkeys.

Beyond the temple is a steep paved but rutted track that leads 800m up to the top of a hill where there is a small ruined **chedi** and, more interestingly, a superb view over the Mekong river and into Laos.

Another kilometre farther along the main road is **Wat Phra That Song Phi Nong**, a temple that has two identical Buddha statues and two identical **chedis** which according to the chronicles were built by two brothers (**song phi nong**).

Chiang Rai to Chiang Mai via Highway 1

As an alternative to returning to Chiang Mai via H 1019, there is the longer but more interesting routing by H 1 which passes through Phayao and Ngao to

Lampang from where H 11 leads back to Chiang Mai.

Phayao. The 89km from Chiang Rai to Phayao pass through mostly flat, monotonous scenery with fields bordering the road and can be covered quickly. The town of Phayao is entered via a turnoff on the right just after KM 741.

Of only minor interest to the casual visitor, Phayao is nevertheless of considerable importance to the historian since it is generally accepted that a settlement existed on the site at least as early as the Bronze Age. It was later abandoned for some reason and not rebuilt until 1096 when Pho Khun Chom Dham re-established it as the capital of a small kingdom, the fine art of which has been linked to that of Chiang Saen. Phayao later allied itself with King Mengrai's Lannathai Kingdom and was eventually absorbed by it.

Limestone Formation, Tham Pha Thai

Lampang

Formerly a district of Chiang Rai, Phayao was raised to the status of a provincial capital in 1977. The town is well sited on the banks of a large lake opposite which looms a 1,700m mountain. It has what the developers like to term 'potential' and plans have been suggested for turning the lake into a tourist attraction by dredging the shallows and using the earth to create an artifical island with recreational facilities. It is likely to be some time before any such plans are put into practice but in the meantime Phayao has two temples worth visiting and certainly deserves at least a brief halt in one's journey.

From the turnoff on H 1 it is 2.6km to **Wat Si Khom Kham** which is situated on the right between the road and the lake. The temple was rebuilt in 1922 and again in 1961 but it is important in that it houses the 400-year-old, 16m high Buddha image of **Phra Chao Ton Luang** which is distinguished by the beautiful sculpting of the face. There is a legend telling how the statue was sculpted by a young couple in return for gold at the prompting of a **naga** king in disguise.

Around the temple courtyard are a few sandstone Buddha heads (sandstone is special to the Phayao style) along with a number of stone tablets inscribed with religious texts. To the right of the **bot** is a garden

105

laid out with a weird mixture of modern concrete statues including, besides Buddhas, mythical creatures, Chinese goddesses and even a dinosaur.

A turning on the right (Chay Kwan Road) 1km beyond the temple leads to the lakeside where there are a few restaurants offering pleasing views out over the water to the mountain beyond.

In the centre of town opposite the local branch of the Bangkok Bank and close to the market is **Wat Luang Raja Santhan**. Possibly dating from the 12th century, this ancient-looking temple has an attractive **viharn** with a roof of wooden tiles supported by teak pillars. Behind are two old **chedis** the smaller of which has a niche enshrining a Buddha image.

Continuing along H 1, the settlement of Ngao is 52km south of Phayao. The road by-passes the town which need not detain the traveller. Just beyond is a turning on the left for H 103 which heads southeast to join H 101 by Rong Kwong and that road leads northeast to Nan (see page 118). This routing permits a visit to the northeastern provinces, described in the following chapter, without returning to Chiang Mai.

H 1 now passes through more interesting scenery with the terrain becoming more hilly and trees and teak plantations taking the place of fields. Near KM KM 673, 12km south of Ngao, a small ruined Burmese-style **chedi** on the right is all that remains of the old Thai Yai monastery complex of **Wat Chong Kham**. This unusual prefabricated wooden structure combining **viharn** and monks' quarters was in danger of falling into total decay but fortunately was saved by being acquired by Muang Boran ('Ancient City'), near Bangkok, where it has been reconstructed and stands today as an excellent example of Northern-style architecture.

Tham Pha Thai. At KM 666.8 a 1km track goes off to the right through a pleasant grove to the base of a cliff where there is the cave of Tham Pha Thai. It is a steep climb up 283 steps to the huge arched entrance to the cave next to which is a **chedi**. Just inside is a Buddha image beside a gigantic stalagmite soaring almost as high as the roof where a hole dramatically spotlights the fantastic formation.

The cave is lit by electric light for its entire 400m length and terminates in a cavern dominated by a large, curiously-shaped chunk of limestone. It is a fascinating walk through the cave, although the visitor should watch his footing as the going is slippery in places.

From here on to Lampang the scenery is quite spectacular as H 1 weaves its way up and around the forested mountains.

Young Elephant Training Centre. A little beyond KM 656 a dirt track on the right leads 1.5km to the Young Elephant Training Centre located near Pang-la village. It is beautifully sited in a saucer-shaped plain surrounded by high rocky hills and, with all the buildings constructed out of natural materials, the Centre blends naturally with its surroundings. The nearby stream of Huay Mae La provides the water for the elephants' daily bath and romp before the rigours of the day begin.

The Centre, the first of its kind, was established in 1969 and is operated by the Veterinary Section of the Northern Timber Work Department, Forest Industry Organization. Its main purpose is to train and discipline young elephants in the skills necessary for working in the government-owned teak forests. In addition a vet is in attendance since elephants, despite their strength and size, are prone to illness and also have to be guarded against snake bites. The tricky task of separating the baby elephant from its mother is further accomplished at the training centre.

Young elephants are enrolled at the age of 3-5 years and their training will take between five and six years. Each animal is first introduced to its **mahout**, or handler, and taught the basic words of command after which it begins more advanced training in the skills of dragging, carrying, pushing and piling up logs, either on its own or with a partner.

The Forest Industry Organization owns some 120 work elephants and there are generally about 7 in each group undergoing training. The Centre is open daily except public holidays (entrance is free) although no classes are held during the hot season (March through May). Demonstrations of elephants learning their skills take place in the early morning from 6 a.m. to 9 a.m. and the 'show' is probably the best of its kind in the North, giving the visitor a good introduction into one of the region's most traditional occupations.

Continuing south on H 1 towards Lampang the road reaches its highest point near KM 650 where it passes between two sheer cliffs. Here on the left is a small shrine and masses of spirit houses at which drivers will blow their horns or **wai** as a mark of respect. Legend has it that the site commemorates the warrior Chao Poh Pratu Pha who fought the Burmese here and although eventually killed remained standing, a sight which apparently scared the invaders away. His spirit is now said to inhabit the hills.

Lampang. A side road on the right just beyond KM 604 enters the provincial capital of Lampang. Spread out on both banks of the Wang river, the town

Portico of Wat Sri Chum, Lampang

can come as a disappointment to anyone who has heard that it is the only place left in Thailand where horse-drawn carriages are still in daily use. It is true that there are carriages, albeit in dwindling numbers, but any idea that such a leisurely mode of transport belonging to a bygone era means that Lampang itself is tranquil and unaffected by the 20th century,' would be totally misleading.

Lampang is located at the junction of H 1, the arterial link between Bangkok and the North, and H 11, the Superhighway to Chiang Mai. Commanding such an important position, the town has developed rapidly during the last couple of decades; concrete shophouses have sprung up and motorized transportation now chokes the narrow streets. The era of the horse-drawn carriage must surely be coming to an end, and if the number of carriages were not decreasing due to lack of proper maintenance facilities (they were originally imported from England during the reign of King Rama VI), they would anyway be soon forced out of existence by the combustion engine.

However, the late arrival of the 20th century has not totally obliterated Lampang's heritage and a number of old traditional houses survive as do several interesting temples. The main problem is finding one's way around.

The old town was built on the right bank of the Wang river, then the centre was switched to the left bank (as it is today) and now expansion is giving rise to development on both banks. All this has produced a highly confusing layout (even with the assistance of a guide from Chiang Mai, the writer managed to get lost more than once) and the traveller is best advised to abandon his car and see the sights by **samlor**, minibus or horse-drawn carriage. The latter charge 20-30 baht for a 15-minute tour around the town centre or an hourly rate of 70-80 baht. The carriage rank is in front of the Government Offices near the market.

Coming from the North, **Wat Chedi Sao** — 'the Temple of the Twenty Chedis' (**sao** is 'twenty' in the northern dialect) — is located outside town on the right bank of the Wang river. It is distinguished by its group of small, white **chedis** in the Burmese style picturesquely located amid lush green rice fields. A small **sala** in the middle of the cluster houses an especially beautifully proportioned sitting Buddha but the nearby modern **viharn** holds no interest. It is the tranquil setting and the impressiveness of the twenty **chedis** that give the temple its charm.

Closer to the town centre but still on the right bank of the river is **Wat Phra Kaeo Don Tao**. This old temple, a mix of Thai and Burmese styles, is dominated by a tall, powerful-looking **chedi** constructed on a stepped rectangular base and rising to a rounded top. Next to the **chedi** is an exquisite 18th century Burmese-style shrine with a many-tiered roof rising to a point and with superbly carved eaves. Inside the ceiling, pillars and back wall are minor masterpieces displaying the skills of the carpenter and woodcarver, as well as being fantastically decorated with coloured glass and enamel inlaid work. The shrine contains three Buddha images.

By the side of this perfect example of Burmese architecture is an old hall built in Thai style with a three-tiered roof and pediments wonderfully enlivened with woodcarving and inlaid coloured glass now faded with age. Inside is a large Sukhothai-style reclining Buddha. Far from clashing, the two distinct forms of the hall and adjacent shrine harmonize perfectly and much of the attraction of the temple is derived from this blending of Thai and Burmese architecture.

Also of interest is the small museum by the left of the gateway which contains fine examples of woodcarving, a number of spirit houses and some old porcelain.

Legend has it that the famous statue of the Emerald Buddha was once lodged at Wat Phra Kaeo Don Tao. It was being brought from Chiang Rai to Chiang Mai by King Sam Fang Kaem in 1436 when the elephant carrying it reached Lampang and refused to go any further. So the statue remained in Lampang until 1468 when King Tilokaraja succeeded in bringing it to his capital in Chiang Mai.

Crossing over to the left bank of the Wang river, there are three temples in the town centre that should not be missed. **Wat Pha Fang**, opposite the Thai Airways office, has a main hall in the Burmese style with a bright green corrugated iron roof although the temple's main attraction is its tall **chedi**. This white structure topped off with gold leaf is surrounded at its base by seven unusual chapels — one for each day of the week — in which there are niches containing statues of the Buddha.

Wat Sri Chum is in pristine condition and is one of the best examples of Burmese architecture. Inside the entranceway the **bot** and **chedi** are on the left and the **viharn** on the right. The roof eaves and pediments of both the main buildings are superbly carved while the **viharn** also has a fine portico and its doors and window shutters are richly decorated, inside and out, with red and gold lacquer.

Inside the **viharn** the ceiling is enlivened with woodcarving and inlaid coloured glass and the supporting pillars are covered with gold and black lacquer. To the right is a bronze Burmese-style Buddha in a glass case. On the opposite wall are red and gold lacquered panels depicting scenes of temples, countryside and, amusingly, two vintage cars.

On the way out can be seen a panel on the inside of the portico where carved figures tell the fable of a young man who looked after his blind parents. One day he was accidently shot by the King who was hunting deer. Angels came to visit the bereaved parents, promising them just one wish, either their son brought back to life or their eyesight restored. They chose their son's life and since they had answered selflessly, not only was their son brought back to them, their eyesight was also restored and they were given gifts of property.

Wat Sri Rong Muang is another Burmese-style temple the exterior of which is visually dazzling. The magnificent roof is covered in white corrugated iron which appears almost silver in the sunlight while the eaves and woodwork are painted in bright yellow, red and blue.

Lampang has a number of good hotels, the most luxurious being the 125-room Tipchang Garnet, and apart from the temples mentioned, the town is worth exploring despite the recent developments. It is still possible to get an idea of what the place must have been like before the 20th century caught up with it, and a ride in one of the horse-drawn carriages should be enjoyed before these symbols of the leisurely past vanish for ever.

For the shopper, Lampang is a noted centre for the production of blue and white pottery and there are some 60 factories in the town which can be visited to see the craftsmen at work and to purchase finished products at better prices than in Chiang Mai or Bangkok.

From Lampang it is just under 100km northwest along H 11 to Chiang Mai. The first 20km pass through flat countryside after which the road enters the hills which separate the valleys of the Ping and Wang rivers. Close to KM 38 there is a mass of spirit houses on the left-hand side, constructed in honour of the spirits who inhabit the hills. Nearby, on the opposite side of the road is a seated bronze Buddha statue.

After KM 59, H 11 flattens out once more and the remainder of the journey to Chiang Mai is unnoteworthy except for the monument to the famous monk, Sri Vichai, which is on the left just after KM 64.

CHIANG MAI TO NAN AND THE EASTERN PROVINCES

Nan and the other eastern provinces are perhaps the least frequented areas of the North although the town of Nan, thanks largely to the attraction of its annual boat races, is beginning to establish itself on the traveller's itinerary. With good roads, fine scenery and a number of towns of note, the popularity of the eastern provinces should increase especially since they can be included, as they are here, on a routing that takes in two of Thailand's most important historical sites, Sukhothai and Si Satchanalai.

For travellers driving up from Bangkok, the eastern provinces are best reached by turning off H 1 onto H 101 at Kamphaeng Phet (see P.152) which is the main highway to Nan, passing through Sukhothai, Si Satchanalai and Phrae.

CITY MAP OF NAN

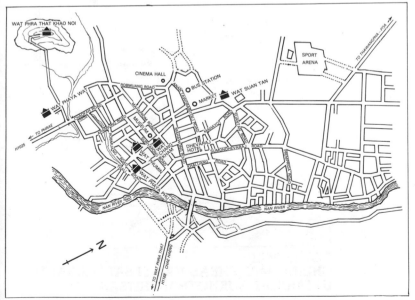

Alternatively, public transport from Chiang Mai to Nan is convenient and plentiful. Four buses a day (at 8.00 a.m., 10.00 a.m., 1.00 p.m. and 3.00 p.m.) leave the northern capital for Nan, taking seven hours to cover the distance. By air there are four Thai Airways flights a week (Mon, Wed, Fri and Sun) from Chiang Mai to Nan, Phrae and Phitsanulok, and three flights a week (Tue, Thur and Sat) that stop at Phrae and Phitsanulok only. Flying time to Nan is 45 minutes.

By car the first leg of the journey from Chiang Mai goes along H 11 to Lampang (see P.109). Going by the number, this same road continues east of H 1 at Lampang although in reality it is not quite that simple. H 11 by-passes Lampang to join H 1; turn left here and travel north along H 1 for 5.6km and then turn right on to H 11 heading southeast. H 11 does cross H 1 but somehow the point of intersection has been pushed out of line so that the west and east sections do not actually join up.

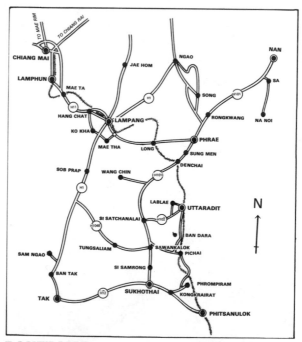

ROUTE MAP:
CHIANG MAI-PHRAE-NAN-SI SATCHANALAI-
UTTARADIT-SUKHOTHAI-PHITSANULOK

Wat Mon San Than. Immediately before the H 11 turnoff a dirt track on the right on H 1 goes up a small hill to Wat Mon San Than. Here there is a typical Burmese-style **viharn**, a gold-topped **chedi** and a white stone **bot** curiously reminiscent of a small church. Inside the latter are traces of mural paintings in poor condition. According to legend the temple was built by a thankful monk on the spot where a giant who was chasing him died, a story that is reflected in the place's other name, **Wat Mon Pu Yak — yak** means 'giant'.

A little farther up the same hill is **Wat Mon Cham Sil** which was built in 1888 although a fire destroyed the **viharn** in 1954 and today, only the **bot** and three interesting Burmese **chedis** remain. A flight of steps leads down the side of the hill at the bottom of which is a stone archway flanked by two stone Burmese lions.

From Highway 1, H 11 runs through a landscape of forested, low-lying hills to join H 101 16km before Den Chai, a small town on the northern railway line from where taxis ply the route to Phrae and Nan. Beyond Den Chai H 101 swings northwards to pass through the fertile valley of the Yom river where one of the principal crops is tobacco and distinctively shaped brick curing houses dot the scenery.

Wat Phra Luang. At KM 123 the road passes the village of Sung Men, just beyond Den Chai, and after 1.9km Wat Phra Luang lies 800m down a turning on the left. Lining this side road are some charming old wooden houses which give a good idea of what Chiang Mai and other typical northern towns must have looked like 50 years or more ago.

The modern **viharn** of the temple is of little interest, apart from containing a fine wooden **thammas**, but to the right is a curious old manuscript repository with a two-tiered roof and two carved porticoed entrances on one side. Behind the **viharn** is a brick **chedi** in Chiang Saen style mixed with Haripunchai influences. There are niches in the four sides housing standing Buddha images and the top of the **chedi** is slightly leaning, giving rise to the temple's local name, **That Nuang** or 'Leaning Relic'.

The exact date of the **chedi** is unknown although it

certainly pre-dates the other buildings and was probably part of a previous temple that was for some reason abandoned. Also of interest is the nearby bell tower, a wooden roofed structure raised on sturdy stone pillars.

Phrae. Returning to H 101, a loop road 5.5km farther on leads 3km left into Phrae. This small but thriving town is not especially attractive and its interest lies in just a few temples displaying Burmese and Laotian architectural styles.

Of the Burmese-style temples **Wat Chom Sawan** is the best example and **Wat Luang** has a good Burmese **chedi. Wat Sra Bo Keo** is a less notable example but its **chedi** is of some interest. Laotian influences are seen in **Wat Si Chum, Wat Pong Sunan, Wat Phra Non** and **Wat Phra Bat Ming Muang Vora Viharn.**

Phrae's most famous temple, **Wat Phra That Cho Hae**, however, is outside the town on a hill 8km to the east. H 1022 goes from the town centre, crosses H 101 and passes through a broad fertile plain to reach the village of **Padang** from where it is 900m to the temple compound.

Two separate flights of stairs lead up the teak-clad hill, the one on the right is more modern looking and has two Burmese lions at the base. The older stairway

Phae Muang Pi

Wat Phaya Wat, Nan

on the left is flanked by **nagas**. Beside the latter is a covered hall containing the reclining Buddha image of **Phra Non** next to which are two statues of seated monks.

At the top of the right-hand stairway is a small shrine housing the revered Buddha image of **Phra Chao Tan Chai** which gives the temple its fame since it is widely regarded as having the power to grant wishes.

Inside the temple's tiny cloister is a 33m high **chedi** covered in gilded copper plates. The **chedi** is squashed up against the walls of the modern **viharn**, interesting because of its cruciform pattern but spoilt by garish decoration and an excessive use of inlaid coloured glass. The mural paintings on the interior walls lack distinction but the red and gold wooden ceiling is quite attractive as is the **thammas.**

Phae Muang Pi. Continuing along H 101 from Phrae, a side road on the right just before KM 143 goes to Phae Muang Pi or 'Ghost City'. The first 1.5km of the road is laterite after which it is surfaced for the 1.7km to the dirt track on the right which covers the remaining 2.7km to Phae Muang Pi. This 'ghost city' is actually a shallow depression in the ground where soil erosion has produced strange chimney-like rock formations that give the impression of weird dwellings on some alien planet.

From the Phae Muang Pi turnoff it is 21km along H 101 to the hamlet of Rong Kwang by KM 163 (note that after the village the kilometre markers for some strange reason drop back into the 50s). Beyond Rong Kwang the highway heads northeast towards Nan and winds its way through gently rolling hills which have been extensively replanted with teak trees. In many places these broad-leaved trees overhang the road producing a shady arbour and the drive throughout is extremely scenic.

Amphoe Sa. After KM 117 (64.6km from Rong Kwang) H 101 descends into the Nan valley and by Amphoe Sa swings left to parallel but not border the river for the remaining 23km to Nan town. At the curve, H 1026 leads straight on to the small settlement of Amphoe Sa.

This sleepy place has one temple worth visiting, **Wat Bun Yeun**, which stands off to the left at the crossroads at the end of the main street. The old **bot** (there is no **viharn**) has a three-tiered roof and a fine, ornate portico with a **garuda** carved on the pediment. The doors, however, are the temple's most striking feature, decorated as they are with two superbly carved guardian figures. Behind the **bot** is a small northern-style **chedi** with statues of a lion, tiger, deer and mythical lion respectively at the corners of the base.

Sao Din. The right-hand turning (H 1026) at the crossroads in Amphoe Sa is a surfaced road that winds its way for 35km to the village of **Na Noi** where nearby are the 'canyons' of Sao Din and Hom Chom — depressions in the ground where soil erosion has produced pillar-like rock formations somewhat similar to a miniature version of the desert canyons of the

American West.

Sao Din is the more impressive of the two sites (it was formerly used as a movie location) and is reached via a turning on the left by Na Noi police station. After 300m turn right at the 'T' junction on to a laterite track that goes 1.6km to a picturesque village of wooden houses built on stilts. Just after the village take the right-hand fork from where it is 2.6km to Sao Din.

Hom Chom lies in the opposite direction to Sao Din and is 1km down the track off to the right by Na Noi police station. Unlike Sao Din, it appears as little more than a worked-out quarry and is scarcely worth the drive although a little farther along the track is a Meo village.

Nan. After retracing one's steps back through Amphoe Sa to H 101, the remainder of the journey to Nan passes through flat countryside with the Nan river unseen off to the right.

Wat Phumin, Nan

One kilometre before the town limits H 1025 branches left from H 101 (signposted 'Khao Noi') and 200m along this side road is **Wat Phaya Wat** on the left. The modern **viharn** contains a Laotian-style **khong phra** that enshrines a seated Buddha. The most interesting feature of the temple, however, is the old **chedi** in the form of a steep pyramid with a stepped base of five tiers each with niches containing Buddha images that display a Sri Lankan influence. The exact date of the **chedi** in unknown and although the statues could indicate construction during the Sukhothai period when Sri Lankan styles were popular, such an age is unlikely.

A short distance from the temple H 1025 rises steeply to wind its way up a lightly wooded hill on top of which is **Wat Phra That Khao Noi**. The **viharn** contains little except a badly painted cement seated Buddha but behind the small white Chiang Saen **chedi**, topped with a gold umbrella, is a **sala** housing two fine Buddha statues in the late Chiang Saen style. The larger one is in the meditation posture while the smaller is in the pose of subduing Mara. These two statues and the fine view of Nan make a trip to the hilltop worthwhile.

Nan, spread out on the west bank of the river of the same name, is a prosperous town judging by its inordinate number of shops selling luxury items. Today, it is a provincial centre although up until as late as the first decade of the 20th century it was the capital of a semi-autonomous principality.

The kingdom of Nan dates from the late 13th century when the Phuka dynasty was founded by Chao Khun Fong, and was first centered on Pua, a few kilometres to the north, until the founding of Nan city in 1368. Its history falls into distinct phases. From the mid-14th century to 1450 there was a close relationship with Sukhothai after which indirect control passed to the Lannathai Kingdom. Then from 1558 to 1786 Nan was under Burmese sovereignty and when those invaders had been expelled, allegiance was pledged to Bangkok in 1788 although the ruling dynasty retained certain privileges until the area came under the full control of the central government in 1931.

Good, first class accommodation is available in the city at the modern Dhevaraj Hotel and at two other smaller properties.

The best starting point for an exploration of Nan is the **National Museum** which is centrally located in what was formerly the Hoh Kam palace built in 1903 by the then ruler Phra Chao Suriyapong Phalitdej. The number of exhibits are few although there is the famous black elephant tusk. This measures 94 cm long and 47 cm in circumference and weighs 18 kg and was supposedly brought to Nan from Chiang Tung by a ruler of the city some 300 years ago.

Yet what the museum lacks in exhibits is made up for by well presented displays of pictures, photographs and texts in English and Thai which give detailed accounts of the city's history, art and major monuments.

Wat Chang Kham Vora Viharn, directly opposite the museum, gets its name from the **chedi**, first built in 1406 but restored several times, which on the second tier of the base is decorated with seven elephant **(chang)** buttresses on each side. The two **viharns** in the temple compound are unexceptional; one formerly housed a walking and a standing Buddha but in 1981 thieves broke in and stole the head from one and the hand from the other and the mutilated statues have subsequently been moved to the museum for safe keeping.

These two images were part of a group of five statues commissioned by the Nan ruler Ngua Ran Pha Sum in 1426. Two of the others are now in Wat Phaya Phu (see below) while the fifth is kept in the monks' residence at Wat Chang Kham Vora Viharn. This image of the walking Buddha is made of pure gold, a fact that was rediscovered by archaeologists Alexander Griswold and Kraisri Nimmanhaeminda in 1955 when the plaster then disguising the statue was broken. Today, this 145cm Buddha is displayed in a glass case and is kept highly polished — proof of the metal's quality but adding nothing to the statue's aesthetic value.

Wat Phumin is on the opposite side of the road about 100m past the traffic lights by Wat Chang Kham Vora Viharn. It is Nan's most notable temple and easily recognised by the two orange coloured lions atop the gateposts. It was built in 1596 by the Nan ruler Phra Chao Chetabutra Phromin and greatly restored in the late 19th century.

The **viharn** follows a cruciform pattern with steps leading up to exquisitely carved entrance doors on each of the four sides. The stairways of the two entrances that parallel the street are flanked by **nagas** with the tail at one doorway and the head at the other. The interior is dominated by a giant centrepiece of four Buddha statues facing the four points of the compass. The walls are decorated with old murals — some restored in recent times which explains the depiction of some **farang** ladies and a steamboat — which tell the story of Chao Kattana Kumara (one of the Buddha's previous lives) and in a fascinating way illustrate detailed scenes of provincial life.

Also of note is the characteristic architecture and fine workmanship of the pillars, rafters and coffered ceiling. The **thammas** again displays excellent qualities.

Wat Phaya Phu. The buildings of Wat Phaya Phu are themselves of little interest and the temple's importance is that it enshrines the other two of the five Buddha statues cast in 1426. Both are made of bronze in the Sukhothai style and both display superb artistry in the poise of the body and serenity of the facial expression. They flank a giant seated Buddha although the larger statue in no way detracts from their aesthetic impact.

Wat Suan Tan, on the western side of town, is distinguished by its 40m high **prang** (rounded spire of Khmer design) instead of the more usual **chedi**. The **viharn** was built in the 15th century but has been restored to the extent that little remains of the original. It does, however, enshrine the important 500-year-old Buddha image of **Phra Chao Thong Tip**. This 4.1m high bronze statue is an excellent example of the Sukhothai style and was commissioned by King Tilokaraja of Chiang Mai in 1449. According to the legend, Tilokaraja, after conquering Nan, gave the people just seven days to collect sufficent metal for the statue and set a 100-day time limit for emigré

Sukhothai artists to cast it.

Wat Phra That Chae Haeng is located southwest of the town on the opposite bank of the Nan river. Following H 1168, it is 1.9km from the bridge to the point where the highway curves left and a broad **naga**-flanked track leads up the small hill to the temple. In the grounds outside the compound are three old chapels and three **chedis** plus, on the left, the entrance to Nan's miniscule zoo.

Wat Phra That Chae Haeng is a walled temple dating from the 11th century and it is held that Lord Buddha once visited the site and predicted that a shrine would be erected there to house sacred relics. The courtyard is dominated by a 55m high **chedi** with four smaller **chedis** and decorative gilded umbrellas at the corners of the base which is surrounded by a terrace and a low, crenellated walls with ornate doorways.

Equally impressive as the **chedi** is the **viharn**, a marvellous structure of Laotian influence with a three-tiered, five level roof. Inside on a fine raised stucco altar is a large seated Buddha with two statues of monks facing it and a row of five other images in front.

One other temple, **Wat Satharos**, on the northern outskirts of town, is also worth visiting. The **viharn** is modern yet its carved door and window shutters show good craftsmanship, but the main point of interest is the unusual **chedi** which has an Ayutthaya-style, bell-shaped top mounted on an abnormally high square base. The small, old **bot** is open-sided with pillars supporting a wooden ceiling and tiled roof. The interior is bare except for two old wooden statues, one seated, the other standing.

Nan's other great attractions are the annual boat races held to celebrate the end of Buddhist Lent (October/November). Taking place along the stretch of river near the Governor's residence, the races are an exceptionally colourful affair with some 40 highly decorated, **naga**-prowed boats and up to 50 oarsmen participating. Each village in the surrounding area sends its own team and its own crowd of enthusiastic supporters who generate wild excitement as the contests get underway. The colour, high spirits and all the fun of the fair make this one of Thailand's most thrilling festivals.

Sirikit Dam. The other major sights of the eastern provinces lie south of Nan and it is necessary to retrace one's steps back along H 101 beyond Phrae before branching left just before Den Chai on to H 1105 which heads south to join H 1045 from where Sirikit Dam lies east and Uttaradit west. Should the traveller wish to omit these places from his itinerary, he can continue along H 101 which leads directly to the ancient site of Si Satchanalai, 80km from the H 1105 turnoff.

H 1105 was completed as a first class road in 1982 and thus offers a good, fast drive. For the first stretch it passes through forested hill country and after 18.7km there is an especially fine view down into the valley on the left. From here the road descends 24km to the Nan valley and joins H 1045 near Ban Ngew Ngam.

At the junction, Uttaradit is 7km to the right along H 1045 while Sirikit Dam is 51km off to the left. On the way to the dam, named after the present Queen of Thailand, the road passes through an attractive wooded area where many young teak trees have been planted as part of the Government's reforestation programme. H 1045 parallels the Nan river but does not actually border it until just before the entrance to the dam site.

Security around Sirikit Dam is rather tight and the first check point comes 1.9km after the road follows the river bank. On the right is a bridge while the dam is straight on. At the Tourist Office 2km farther along is another check point where the visitor must register and obtain a permit. (For those in need of refreshment there is a food stall opposite the office — something worth remembering since there are only drink stalls at the crest of the dam.)

Half a kilometre past the Tourist Office the road turns right and crosses the river. Turn left at the end of the bridge from where it is 400m to the third check point and then 800m up the hill to the crest of the dam.

Sirikit Dam is the largest earth wall dam in Thailand being 810m long, 113.6m high and 12m wide. The lake behind covers 269 sq km and is bordered by low forested hills. In addition to providing electricity and irrigation to the region, the lake is also well stocked with fish and provides a source of livelihood to villagers living around the banks. It is a picturesque spot although, unfortunately, there are no good roads for visiting the little fishing villages nor as yet are there any boats for hire. One can view the dam, admire the scenery and have a drink at the picnic stalls, but that is all until some recreational facilities are developed.

Should the traveller wish to stay overnight, there is a guesthouse with 21 air-conditioned rooms (120 baht for a single, 180 baht double) and nine rooms with fan (80 baht single and 120 baht double).

Inside Wat Phra Tan Sila At

World's Largest Teak Tree. Located not far from Sirikit Dam in **Sak Yai National Park** is what is claimed to be the world's oldest and tallest teak tree. From the entrance to the dam site turn left over the bridge across the Nan and then left on to H 1146. At the junction after 11.4km turn right on to H 1047 (unsurfaced) and then right again after 6.9km on a narrow track that leads 1.3km to a pleasant grove on the left.

The venerable teak tree, set apart by a small wooden fence, is said to be over 1,000 years old and its circumference at its base measures 9.7m and, in 1970, its height was put at 47m although a high wind in 1977 snapped off a small portion of the top.

Wat Phra Fang. Returning back along H 1045 towards Uttaradit, Wat Phra Fang (Wat Sawang Buri Munee Nad) is located just before the town on the opposite bank of the Nan river. At the junction of H 1045 and H 1105 turn left and 900m beyond the bridge over the river, turn right onto H 11008 which after 7km passes the village of **Ban Had Suaten** (marked by large factory on the right). Just beyond, the road deteriorates into a dirt track and after 4.3km reaches the temple which lies off to the left in a tree-shaded spot on the river bank.

The **viharn** dates from the Sukhothai period and is partially ruined yet massive pillars still support what remains of the roof. Inside there is a large seated Buddha statue. The modern **bot** houses a fine Chiang Saen-style bronze Buddha — **Ong Phra Fang** — and behind the **viharn** is an old **chedi** raised on a stepped base and surrounded by a low wall. A little way off stands an ancient meditation hall and an old **bot** that still has some stucco decoration around the window frames.

Uttaradit. Returning to the right bank of the Nan, H 1045 leads into the centre of Uttaradit. During the Ayutthaya period the town had great strategic importance being on the border of the northern territories then under Burmese control and it is famous for its local hero Phraya Phichai Dabhak who successfully fought off a Burmese invasion during the reign of King Taksin after the fall of Ayutthaya.

A monument to Phraya Phichai stands near the provincial offices but apart from that there is little in Uttaradit to remind the traveller of its past. Situated between the railway line and the river, the town was badly damaged by fire in 1967 and the new concrete buildings that have sprung up lack character. Nevertheless, the river frontage does add some charm to the place which today is mostly noted for the quality of its **durian** and **langsad** fruit.

Wat Tha Thanon. Apart from Wat Phra Fang mentioned above, there are three other temples just outside of Uttaradit on the way to Si Satchanalai worth visiting, but in the town centre the only real attraction is Wat Tha Thanon on the street facing the river.

Just inside the temple gates is a small, arched-roofed, Chinese-style chapel that is ornate and colourful and enshrines the revered image of **Luang**

Wat Chang Lom,
Si Satchanalai

Po Phet, a fine bronze seated Buddha in Chiang Saen style. The modern **bot** to the left is unremarkable except for its window shutters which are decorated with gilded carvings of **kilane**, a mythical creature with the head of a dragon and the body of a horse.

Wat Phra Boromathat. From the southern end of Uttaradit H 102 swings west to join H 101 near Si Satchanalai 40km away. At KM 5 on the left is Wat Phra Boromathat, an old temple that has been much restored so that from the outside it looks almost new except for its characteristic deep, low-roofed porticos at the front and back. Inside the **viharn** the age of the temple is more apparent. The roof is supported by twin rows of four pillars and there are the remains of mural paintings above the door. A large, gilded seated Buddha in the Sukhothai style plus a number of smaller images decorate the interior.

Behind the **viharn** is an old **chedi** mounted on a square base with four smaller **chedis** at the corners. Traces of Sri Lankan influences date construction from the Sukhothai period although much restoration was carried out during Ayutthaya times.

Wat Phra Yeun Phra Bat Yukon. One kilometre beyond Wat Phra Boromathat H 102 curves to the right while a short track goes straight on up a small hill to Wat Phra Yeun Phra Bat Yukon. Of principal interest here is the unusual **mondop** which has a multi-tiered, pyramid-shaped roof raised on a series of columns. Inside are one standing and two seated Buddhas in Sukhothai style plus, in the centre, a Buddha footprint in a raised lotus-shaped surround. Behind the **mondop** are three badly ruined **chedis.**

Wat Phra Tan Sila At. A hundred metres away on the same hilltop is Wat Phra Tan Sila At which dates from the Ayutthaya period although the **viharn** is modern, replacing the original that was destroyed by fire in 1908. Inside is an ornate centrepiece over a depression in the ground where Lord Buddha is said to have sat. Also of note are the door and window shutters which are deeply and richly carved.

At the back is a beautiful collection of bronze and gold leaf-covered statues, the most famous of which are the five small seated Buddhas in front, named **Phra**

Siang Tai. Legend holds that if a person has strong spiritual belief he can make these images rise in the air.

To the side of the **viharn** are two small chapels; the one on the left containing a Buddha footprint in bronze. In front and slightly to the left of the **viharn** is a superb old, two-storeyed teak **sala** with a carved pediment on the top tier of the roof.

Si Satchanalai. From these two temples H 102 continues straight to join H 101 north of the ancient city of Si Satchanalai. Turn left onto the highway which parallels the Yom river and 11.5km south (near KM 18) a turning on the right leads 600m to a bridge over the river from where a laterite track goes left and right to the monuments of Si Satchanalai. To arrive at the ancient site in more traditional style there is a crossing point a little before the bridge where small boats ferry passengers across the Yom.

Si Satchanalai was founded in the 13th century at the same time as Sukhothai, the capital of the first Thai kingdom. The former was generally referred to as the twin city of the latter and was usually governed by a son of the Sukhothai king. In some respects Si Satchanalai today is more impressive than its 'twin' to the south. It is, of course, much smaller and its buildings were not designed on such a grand scale as those at Sukhothai, but its compactness makes it easier for the modern visitor to get an impression of its former glory. And that impression is enhanced by the location of the city on a small hill that is now pleasantly wooded, and by the strange air of sanctity that pervades the tranquil setting.

The old walled city and major monuments lie along the track leading off right after the bridge. 500m along the path on the left are the ruins of **Wat Khok Singa Ram** where there are the remains of the columns and walls of the **viharn** behind which are three round **chedis**. Another kilometre farther along, a track on the left leads 200m up the hill to the heart of the city (entrance 2 baht).

The first of the major monuments to be seen is **Wat Chang Lom**, the 'temple surrounded by elephants', as recorded by King Ramkamhaeng in his famous stone inscription found at Sukhothai, and most likely constructed by him in the late 13th century. Columns of the small **viharn** survive although it is the large bell-shaped **chedi** that is of most interest and which gives the temple its name. It stands on a square base decorated originally with 39 elephant buttresses of which many remain somewhat disfigured. The upper tier of the base has niches to enshrine Buddha images, some still in place.

Directly southeast of Wat Chang Lom are the ruins of **Wat Chedi Chet Thaew**. These extensive remains are distinguished by the seven **(chet)** rows of **chedis** probably built to contain the ashes of members of the Sukhothai dynasty who ruled the city. Of special note is the **chedi** facing Wat Chang Lom on which there is a reasonably well preserved stucco Buddha seated on a **naga**.

Walking Buddha,
Sukhothai Museum

Wat Mahathat, Sukothai

Continuing in a southeasterly line are the ruins of **Wat Uthayan Yai** and **Wat Nang Phaya**, the western wall of the latter's **viharn** still having some partially intact stucco decoration dating from the Ayutthaya period.

To the northwest of the city are the ruins of **Wat Khao Phanom Pleung** and **Wat Khao Suwan Kiri**, each picturesquely sited atop a small hill from where there are fine views of the ancient city in its entirety.

Perhaps the most impressive of all the monuments in the vicinity is **Wat Phra Si Ratana Mahathat** which lies some way east of the city proper at Chaliang, close to the banks of the Yom river about 1km to the left after crossing the bridge. Set out in a west-east line, the remains comprise two seated Buddhas, a large Sri Lankan-style cone-shaped **chedi**, a beautiful **prang**, a large brick and stucco seated Buddha, a standing Buddha partially embedded in the ground and, finally, the columns of the main **viharn**.

The temple was most likely built in the late 13th century by King Ramkamhaeng but was restored in Ayutthaya times which explains why the upper section of the **prang** shows Khmer influence, the architectural style that was then again popular. The whole of the **prang** is a most impressive structure yet the temple's special claim to fame is the high-relief laterite and stucco walking Buddha which is a masterpiece of its kind. The carved wooden doors of the **prang** and part of the ceiling decoration can be seen today in the Ramkamhaeng National Museum at Sukhothai and give a good indication of the temple's original magnificence.

Not only an impressive city, Si Satchanalai was also famous for its pottery when, during the reign of King Ramkamhaeng, craftsmen from China were brought to Sukhothai and later to Sawankhalok (former name of Si Satchanalai) where the quality of the clay was better. Sawankhalok ceramics, distinguished by their light grey colour, often tinged with blue or green, represented a high point in local handicrafts and were important export items. Examples of these wares (some possibly antique although of poor quality) can be purchased at the few stalls that line the track on the way to Si Satchanalai near Wat Khok Singa Ram.

Sukhothai. From the turnoff to Si Satchanalai H 101 heads south to join H 12. From the junction the modern town of Sukhothai lies 1.7km to the left. It is an exceptionally unattractive collection of concrete shophouses although there are a few reasonable hotels which make the town a base for visiting the ancient city of Sukhothai, some 12km to the west along H 12.

Old Sukhothai (the name literally means 'Dawn of Happiness') was probably originally founded in the 12th century at which time the Thais were scattered about the area in separate villages while invaders from the powerful Khmer kingdom held sway. Then, in the early 13th century, two Thai chiefs, Phor Khun Pha Muang and Phor Khun Bang Klang Thao, joined forces and led their people to a victory over the Khmers, forcing them out of Sukhothai and, in 1238, establishing the city as the capital of the first Thai kingdom under the rule of King Sri Intratit who established the Phra Ruang dynasty.

The newly independent kingdom flourished rapidly and was vastly expanded to unite the Thai people. The zenith of its power and the full flowering of its culture was achieved during the reign of King Ramkamhaeng, now known as Ramkamhaeng the Great, who ruled from 1279 to 1299.

By the 15th century Sukhothai had lost its autonomy and was appended to Ayutthaya, the capital of the new

Thai kingdom located much farther south in the valley of the Chao Phya river. The city was finally abandoned in the 16th century and was never revived although its influence on Thai art and technology was for long to remain strong.

Today, the Sukhothai Historical Park covers 70 sq km and occupies a peaceful, stately setting of well maintained lawns, ponds and, in the background, wooded hills. Moreover, the monuments have recently undergone extensive restoration so that the glory that was Sukhothai is far from fading.

Within the city walls there are more than 20 major monuments while many more are scattered in all directions beyond the old fortifications. At least a full day, therefore, is needed to do the site justice and to gain a full appreciation. Below are described only the most important monuments that should be included in even the briefest visit.

H 12 cuts directly east-west through the centre of old Sukhothai and the city is first announced by the eastern ramparts — the former Kamphaenghak Gate — between which the road passes. These fortifications are part of the original defences that included three rows of walls and moats and reflect the then military policy of letting the enemy come to you. In fact Sukhothai never did fall as the last ruler surrendered to Ayutthaya at Kamphaeng Phet.

River at Phitsanulok

A few hundred metres beyond the gate on the left is
Ramkamhaeng National Museum, the best starting
point for exploring the site. Open Wednesday to
Sunday (entrance is free except for 2 baht on Saturday
and Sunday), the museum covers two storeys and
contains a superb collection of Sukhothai sculpture
and other artifacts found at the three main cities of the
kingdom — Sukhothai, Si Satchanalai and Kamphaeng
Phet. Exhibits representing the art of other periods are
also on display.

Of all the exhibits perhaps the most magnificent is
the statue of a walking Buddha that is displayed to
superb effect just inside the entrance. This style of
image in the round, as opposed to relief, was an
innvoation of Sukhothai artists and the sense of poise,
grace and serenity effected by the sculptors mark these
statues as the crowning glory of the art of the period.

Also of special note is the copy of King
Ramkamhaeng's famous stone inscription, the original

*Phra Buddha
Chinaraj, Phitsanulok*

of which is now in the National Museum in Bangkok. Discovered in 1833 by the then Crown Prince Mongkut, the stone, inscribed in 1292, records the conquests and achievements made during the reign of King Ramkamhaeng. It was originally at the **Noen Phrasat**, or Palace Mound, near Wat Mahathat, and was found together with a piece of the stone throne, on which the king sat when conducting affairs of state.

Wat Mahathat. Some 300m west of the museum along a laterite path are the ruins of the Royal Palace and Wat Mahathat which mark the centre of the old walled city. Wat Mahathat is the largest and most famous of Sukhothai's temples and its magnificent architecture is distinguished by the central **chedi** in lotus bud shape which is peculiar to the Sukhothai period. It stands on a large platform surrounded by four brick **stupas** at the corners and four laterite Khmer **prangs**. The base of the platform is decorated with stucco figures of Buddhist disciples while stucco work on the **prangs** depict scenes from the life of Buddha and display a Sri Lankan influence.

The temple was most likely founded by King Sri Intratit but was extensively remodelled during the reign of King Loe Thai in the early 14th century. It was during the latter time that Buddhism of the Sri Lankan school found favour at Sukhothai and its influence can be traced in the religious architecture of the period.

Two giant restored standing Buddhas, partially enclosed by surrounding walls, flank the **chedi** while from the eastern approach is the best known view of Wat Mahathat with the twin rows of the **viharn's** pillars and the large restored seated Buddha high on a brick platform, all of which are of later date than the main chedi.

Wat Sri Sawai. Located southwest of Wat Manhathat is Wat Sri Sawai, easily distinguished by its three Khmer-style laterite **prangs** and surrounding laterite walls. The temple was probably first founded in the late 12th or early 13th century but was left unfinished until the 15th century when the stucco work must have been added. In 1908, the Crown Prince, later King Rama VI, discovered part of a Hindu sculpture at the site and it was his opinion that the temple was once a shrine to Siva before being converted into a Buddhist monastery. A record of his discovery is inscribed on a stone tablet outside the northern wall of the compound.

Wat Trapang Ngoen lies west of Wat Mahathat on a small island in the middle of a pool known as Silver Lake. In addition to the remains of the columns of the **viharn** there is also a fine **chedi** which is picturesquely framed by the hills in the background, a sight further enhanced by its reflection in the water.

North of Wat Mahathat is **Wat Chana Songkhram**, noted for its main round **chedi** and the bases of smaller **chedis** all in Sri Lankan style. Slightly farther north and to the west is **Wat Sra Sri**. This is a superb monument with a Sri Lankan-style **chedi** and the ruins of a **viharn** on an island in the pond of Traphang Trakuan. In front are the remains of a large **viharn** containing a stucco Buddha image.

The above are the major monuments to be seen inside the city walls while the following are the most important of the ruins scattered farther afield around Sukhothai Historical Park.

Wat Phra Phai Luang. About 1km beyond the northern gate, **Pratu San Luang**, is Wat Phra Phai Luang the extensive remains of which are second in importance only to Wat Mahathat. It most likely dates from the period of Khmer occupation and originally had three **prangs** similar to those of Wat Sri Sawai but only one is still standing. In front of the **prang** are the ruins of a **viharn** and a **chedi**, the base of the latter being decorated with stucco seated Buddhas. Nearby is a **mondop** containing Buddha images in the postures of standing, sitting, walking and reclining.

Wat Si Chum lies southwest of Wat Phra Phai Luang and features a massive square **mondop** which enshrines one of Thailand's largest seated Buddhas in the posture of subduing Mara. The image, named in King Ramkamhaeng's inscription as **Phra Achana**, is 11.3 m wide at the lap while the surrounding **mondop** 11.3m wide at the lap while the surrounding **mondop** is 32m square and 15m high. The walls are 3m thick left wall, the ceiling of which is decorated with engraved slabs illustrating scenes from the Buddhist

Jataka tales. Unfortunately, this passageway is currently closed to the public although some of the engravings can be glimpsed through the bars of the gate.

Apart from the magnificence of its statue, Wat Si Chum is also important in Thai history as it was here, in 1577, that King Naresuan the Great of Ayutthaya received the oath of allegiance from his army while on an expedition to subdue rebels at Sawankhalok.

Wat Saphan Hin is located about 2km west of the city atop a small hill off to the left of H 12 in the direction of Tak. This temple of 'Stone Bridge' gets its name from the slate slab pathway leading up the 50m hill. Inside the **viharn**, of which only the laterite columns remain, is a 12.5m tall Buddha image with its right hand raised in the attitude of giving protection. From the hilltop there is a good view of the surrounding countryside.

Of the group of monuments south of the city, the most important is **Wat Chetupon** of which a **mondop** was the main sanctuary. Only the back wall remains standing where there are Buddha images in the walking, standing, sitting and reclining postures. Portions of the gates and outer walls constructed of slate can still be seen while in front of the mondop are the remains of a large **viharn**. Behind the **mondop** is a small sanctuary enshrining a Buddha image known locally as **Phra Sri Ariya (Maitreya)**, 'the Buddha of the future'.

To the east of the city, the most important monument is **Wat Chang Lom**, a bell-shaped Sri Lankan-style **chedi** raised on a square base supported by now disfigured elephant buttresses.

Phitsanulok. Southeast of new Sukhothai, 58km along H 12 is the important communications and commercial centre of Phitsanulok. The journey passes through flat countryside which, although there is nothing in the terrain to suggest it, separates the valleys of the Yom and Nan rivers. Phitsanulok is located on the left bank of the latter which is spanned by a modern concrete bridge.

The town lies on the borderline of the Central and Northern regions and as such has historically held strategic and political importance, especially during the Ayutthaya period when it was a recruiting and rallying ground for armies on expeditions against the Burmese-occupied North. Phitsanulok is also famous as the birthplace of King Naresuan.

Evidence of the town's long and rich past, however, was largely destroyed by a great fire some years ago and today the modern buildings are monotonous in their concrete uniformity and tasteless in design. Nevertheless, Phitsanulok is saved from unremitting ugliness by the Nan river, a busy communications link. Its banks are pleasantly tree-lined and the string of moored houseboats and rafts on both sides add, if not colour, at least character in their representation of traditional riverine life.

Phitsanulok has three good air-conditioned hotels, making it a convenient overnight stop, and apart from the attraction of the river, there are three temples worth visiting, one of which contains a highly revered Buddha image.

Wat Phra Sri Mahathat. Phitsanulok's most famous landmark, Wat Phra Sri Mahathat, faces the river on the left of the bridge coming into town. Fortunately the temple was unscathed by the fire and stands as a superb monument with its central, gilded **prang** in Khmer style dominating the skyline.

Giving rise to the temple's fame is the Buddha image of **Phra Buddha Chinaraj** which is enshrined in the main chapel and daily attracts hundreds of devotees. Such veneration has had the unfortunate side-effect of giving rise to a lively trade in religious objects and other souvenirs although even this bustle cannot detract from the stunning beauty of the central image.

Dating from the 14th century, the highly polished bronze statue of the seated Buddha is an excellent example of late Sukhothai art, the characteristics of which are noticeable in the fingers of equal length, the exaggerated curve of the overlapped legs and the somewhat rounded, serious face. The image, of which many copies exist, the best known being in Bangkok's Marble Temple, has a halo surrounding the head and shoulders and the whole statue is stunningly set off by a black backdrop decorated with gilded angels and flowers.

The impact of the central image is further heightened by the architecture of the **bot** which is a fine example of the traditional three-tiered roof with low-sweeping eaves which from the inside have the effect of diminishing the side walls. This results in an accentuation of the nave and the focussing of attention on the statue at the end.

There are other fine Buddha images on both sides of the main statue and, in front, are two very beautiful wooden **thammas**. Also of great interest are the doors of the chapel which, constructed in 1756, are fantastically decorated with inlaid mother-of-pearl on a black background. On the inside walls either side of the doorway are restored mural paintings depicting, on the left, the Buddha story of Phra Vessandon Chadok and, on the right, scenes from episodes in the Buddha's life.

In the cloisters and chapels surrounding the principal shrine are collections of Buddha statues, ceramics and other artifacts some of which are of great value although they are exhibited in such a cluttered fashion as to hinder full appreciation.

At the back of the temple compound is an open area which offers the best prospect of the central **prang** that was built in the Ayutthaya period. Here there are also the remains of 10 laterite columns, all that survives of an earlier **viharn**, and a tall standing Buddha which has been restored and looks rather too freshly painted.

Wat Raja Burana. Directly to the right of the bridge over the Nan river on the opposite side of the road is Wat Raja Burana, marked by its large, partially ruined **chedi** raised on a massive brick base. To the right is a small manuscript repository built up on sturdy stone pillars between which hangs a temple bell.

The dilapidated **viharn** behind the **chedi** is empty but the small, old **bot** beyond should not be missed. It is generally kept locked but the abbot will open it on request. Inside there are twin rows of five solid pillars supporting the roof yet the resulting confined space still manages to contain a large seated Buddha with several other interesting images behind it. The walls are covered with mural paintings in comparatively good condition depicting scenes from the **Ramayana**.

Phitsanulok's other main monument, **Wat Chulamani**, lies 5km south of the town along H 1063. This temple is now partially ruined although the main laterite building with its Khmer-style **prang** was well restored by the Fine Arts Department in 1954; the original itself having been much reconstructed by King Boromtrailokanat of Ayutthaya in the late 15th century. This monarch was the first of the Ayutthaya rulers to take control of the domains of old Sukhothai and while viceroy of Phitsanulok made a study of the history and customs of the first Thai kingdom.

Today, the main doorway and steep steps of the temple are in good condition and the two side entrances still have original stucco work surrounds. On parts of the outer wall traces of a stucco frieze of running geese are also readily apparent.

In front of the temple is a large stone seated Buddha flanked by two monks. Behind is an old brick building with, on one side, a restored stucco Buddha over two wooden shutters that protect a stone inscription dating from the time of King Narai and stating that King Boromtrailokanat was ordained as a monk here.

Returning from Phitsanulok to Sukhothai, one can either continue along H 12 which joins H 1 by Tak, or take H 101 which heads southwest from Sukhothai to Kamphaeng Phet. For descriptions of these two places see following chapter.

CHIANG MAI TO TAK AND BEYOND

T ak, some 280km south of Chiang Mai and 420km north of Bangkok, is generally accepted as being the gateway to the North. This was certainly the case in the past when armies from Ayutthaya used the town as a staging post during expeditions against the Lannathai kingdom.

However, although Tak can trace its history far back, no ruins of any significance remain to bear witness to its heritage, and the town's importance lies in its being an ideal base for the traveller. Within easy reach are the ancient sites of Sukhothai and Kamphaeng Phet to the east and southeast respectively, while to the west lie hilltribe villages and the Burmese border, and just north is Bhumipol Dam and the scenic Mae Ping lake.

RUINS MAP OF SUKHOTHAI

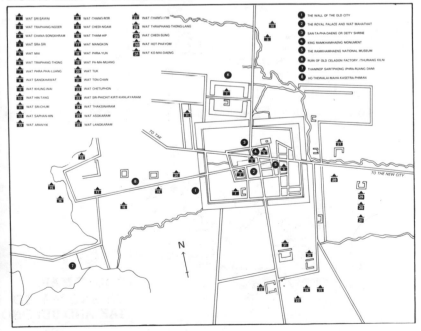

Situated on Highway 1 and with first class accommodation available at the Viang Tak Hotel, Tak is often used as an overnight stop for those driving up from Bangkok to Chiang Mai. Should the traveller be making this trip, the directions given here can be taken in reverse order.

The first stage of the journey south from Chiang Mai follows H 11 to Lampang (see P.109), where one turns right on to H 1.

Wat Phra That Lampang Luang. Close to KM 588 (distance from Bangkok) on H 1, 9.5km south of the Lampang turnoff, a side road on the right leads 1.4km to the village of **Ko Kha** just beyond which is the important temple of Wat Phra Lampang Luang. Continue through the settlement, across the bridge over the Wang river then turn right at the 'T' junction from where it is 3km to the temple which stands on a small hill on the left-hand side of the road.

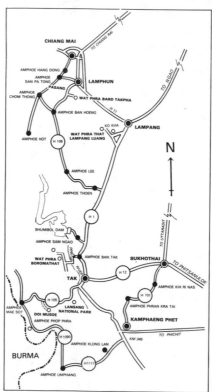

**ROUTE MAP:
CHIANG MAI TO
TAK AND BEYOND**

CITY MAP OF TAK

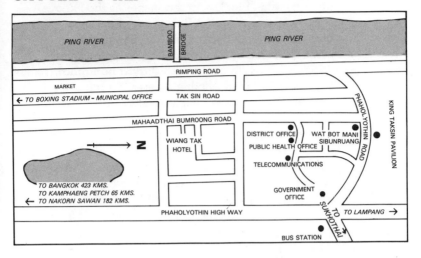

The compound is impressively walled, a reminder of its former role as a stronghold and the important part it played in the history of the area for which it is still highly revered. It is believed that a **wat** was originally constructed on the site in 496 by King Prajao Sri Thatta but it was completely rebuilt in the 18th century. And it was at that time that the event for which Wat Lampang Luang is most famous took place.

It was in 1736 that Tao Maha Yote, Chief Commander of Lamphun, then under Burmese control, was shot at the temple by Tip Chaang, the ruler of Lampang. The Burmese had temporarily occupied the **wat** and believed themselves safe from attack but Tip Chaang by-passed the fortifications and gained access to the compound via a drainage tunnel that can still be seen. As a record of the ensuing fight is a hole in one of the iron railings surrounding the main **chedi** reputedly caused by a bullet fired by Tip Chaang.

A **naga**-flanked flight of steps lead up to the temple's massive main gates but these are generally locked and the usual way in today is by the steps up the left side of the compound.

At the top of the steps outside the main walls is a large bo tree with its ancient branches supported by many props. At the far end of the courtyard is a building protected by an iron grill gate and housing

143

an 'emerald' Buddha image said to have been carved from the same block of green jasper as the famous statue in Bangkok's Wat Phra Kaeo. Nearby is a tiny museum with a collection of Buddha images, 10th-12th century sandstone Buddha heads, carved wooden thrones, 16th-17th century **khakayia bongphai** (rocket launcher) and several other interesting relics.

In the centre of the temple compound proper is a **chedi** in Lannathai style with a square base and covered in tin and copper plates which are finished off in gold leaf at the top. Between the **chedi** and the main gates is the **viharn** which, although a fine example of northern architecture, is made somewhat less impressive today by a newly re-tiled roof.

The inside is dominated by twin rows of 10 massive pillars supporting the roof while the upper panels of the half-open sides are decorated with badly weathered murals. Of principal interest is the tall, ornate, gilded cabinet that encases the venerated image of **Phra Chao Laan Thong**. To the left of this is an antique wooden **thammas**; to the right and behind are a collection of Buddha images.

To the left of the **chedi** is the **bot** but this is usually locked, nevertheless it is pleasant to stroll around the compound where there is much to see, notably the famous drainage tunnel, and a strong sense of history is inescapable.

CITY MAP OF KAMPHAENG PHET

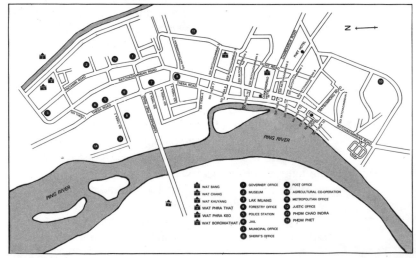

Wat Phra Boromathat, near Ban Tak

Returning back through Ko Kha to H 1, the road continues south through surrounding scenery of low-lying forested hills. Just before KM 515 a turning on the right leads into the small town of **Thoen** which lies on a loop road off H 1 at the junction with H 106, the old Chiang Mai road. There is little to detain the traveller here and the place's only slight reputation rests on its **pohng kham** 'lucky' stones. These are a form of quartz with coloured impurities embedded, making strange patterns.

Bhumipol Dam. At KM 463 there is a turnoff on the right signposted Sam Ngao 15km and Bhumipol Dam 17km. A little way along this side road there is a curious sign warning of low flying aircraft. Nearby there is an airstrip for light planes serving the workings at the dam.

Before reaching Bhumipol Dam there are two turnings on the left, one after 11.9km and the other after 13.2km, that enter the hamlet of Sam Ngao. This is basically an uninteresting village of small wooden houses strung out along the bank of the Ping river. However, there are three Buddha images that give the place its name on the opposite bank of the river about 3km down a dirt track to the right after crossing the Chama Devi bridge.

The dam area itself lies 2.6km beyond Sam Ngao and is virtually a small town in its own right, comprising as it does a colony of bungalows most of which are for EGAT (Electricity Generating Authority of Thailand) employees, although some are also for rent. The main hotel, however, is the 26-room 'Guesthouse 100' which is attractively sited on the banks of the river a little way downstream from the dam wall. A nearby 18-hole golf course adds to the attractions. Permission to use the links or to visit the dam itself must be obtained from the hotel reception. (For those not staying at the guesthouse there is an information centre on the right 800m past the main entrance to the site.)

The crest of the dam is 4.8km from the guesthouse and blocks the Ping river at a point where there is a natural narrows formed by the surrounding hills.

Bhumipol Dam, named after Thailand's present King but also referred to as Yanhee Dam, is Thailand's largest concrete dam having a 486m long curved crest, a maximum height of 154m and a maximum

Ban Tak

thickness of 52.2m. Preliminary construction work was begun in 1957 and in 1961 the foundation stone was laid by King Bhumipol. The first two turbines came into operation in 1964 and another five have subsequently been brought into use while there is still provision for an eighth.

In addition to generating 553,000 kilowatts of electricity, the dam also provides irrigation in the dry season downstream in Tak and Kamphaeng Phet provinces and the Chao Phya plain while in the rainy season it reduces flood hazard in those areas. The spillway of two 500m long tunnels is capable of discharging 6,000 cu m per second which is equivalent to the flood magnitude occuring approximately once in every 1,000 years.

Behind the dam the Mae Ping lake covers an area of 318 sq km and holds 13,462 million cu m of water. The lake, scenically surrounded by forested hills, stretches 207km north as far as the town of Hot. Arrangements can be made at the guesthouse for hiring small boats (taking up to 15 persons) at a rate of 550 baht per hour reducing to 450 baht for the second and subsequent hours. Larger vessels for tours along the entire length of the lake up to Doi Tao can be chartered from the Chiang Mai Lake Tour Company which has offices in Chiang Mai and Bangkok.

The fascination of the dam, the beauty and tranquillity of the scenery and the good facilities of the guesthouse make at least a one-night stay well worthwhile.

Ban Tak. From the turnoff to Bhumipol Dam H 1 continues south for 20.4km before reaching a loop road on the right which enters the small hamlet of Ban Tak on the banks of the Ping. From H 1 turn left at the 'T' junction after 200m and then right after 400m into the main street which leads down to the river.

There are actually two Ban Taks, **Ok** and **Tok** meaning 'east' and 'west', covering both banks of the river and connected by a rickety 600m wooden bridge. It is a simple but extremely picturesque spot with old wooden houses built on stilts at the water's edge, children playing joyfully in the river, women washing clothes by the banks — in fact every aspect of traditional daily riverine life that has changed hardly at all over the years.

Ban Tak Tok on the far bank is the more attractive of the two sections of the village and few kilometres beyond are two important historical monuments.

Wat Phra Boromathat. After crossing the bridge into Ban Tak Tok turn right and follow the river bank for 500m then take first left and first right on to H 1107 that passes between paddy fields. Turn left after 2.6km on to a dirt road (H 1175) and 400m later a short track on the left leads directly to a flight of **naga**-flanked steps that go up to Wat Phra Boromathat.

The precise history of the temple is unknown although it is believed that a **wat** was first built on the site in 503 BC. However, with the exception of an old dilapidated **viharn** situated behind the **chedi** and containing a small reclining Buddha, the buildings in the compound are comparatively modern.

The **chedi** is the most interesting feature and is entirely covered in gold leaf and surrounded by smaller **chedis** and tiny spired 'houses' with Buddha images inside. The present structure was built about 60 years ago over the site of the original **chedi** which was said to have enshrined the Buddha relics of four hairs and part of the right hand.

1.4km farther along H 1175 a track on the right goes a couple of hundred metres to a Sukhothai-style **stupa** with a square base and rounded top. This marks the spot where, in 1262, Prince Ramkamhaeng, later to become King Ramkamhaeng the Great of Sukhothai, at the age of 19 saved the life of his father, King Intratit. The latter, while attempting to consolidate and expand his new-found kingdom of Sukhothai, was forced into battle with the Prince of Chot who was trying to capture Tak and take over leadership of the Thai people. Seeing his father's life in danger, Prince Ramkamhaeng charged his elephant at that ridden by the Prince of Chot and entered into single combat, the first on elephant back recorded in Thai history. Ramkamhaeng defeated Chot and forced him and his army to flee. The **stupa** was constructed to commemorate the victory although some historians doubt if the one seen today is the original.

For some obscure reason, four green-painted concrete statues of soliders standing to attention have been set up behind the **stupa**. These are crude and ugly and tend to defeat any attempt by the visitor to conjure up a vision of Ramkamhaeng's moment of glory.

Tak. The modern town of Tak is situated 23.5km south of Ban Tak on H 1. The main highway skirts the eastern side of the town before swinging west just beyond Tak to cross the Ping river and continue south paralleling its right bank. There are several side roads leading into the town centre, the most northerly being by KM 422 at the junction with H 12 which leads left 80km to Sukhothai and right into Tak which is strung out along the left bank of the river.

There is nothing in the appearance of the town to suggest it, but the whole area around Tak is steeped in history. Between 243 BC and 17 AD there was a Thai Yai (Shan) kingdom here while in the 7th century it is believed that Queen Chama Devi passed through the region when travelling up the Ping river to ascend the throne of Haripunchai (Lamphun). Following the battle of Ban Tak mentioned above and the Sukhothai period, Tak was a northern border town of the Ayutthaya kingdom and as such held considerable strategic importance.

It is from the latter part of the Ayutthaya period in the 18th century that Tak, or at least its name, has some claim to fame. In 1734, a boy was born in the capital of Ayutthaya to a Chinese father and a Thai mother. Early in life he fell under the patronage of a nobleman and was given the name Sin, meaning 'money' or 'property.' He quickly rose in royal favour and was eventually made governor of Tak and given the title Phya Tak.

He was later to fight with distinction during the defence of Ayutthaya against the Burmese and when that city fell in 1767 he managed to flee south, rally the Thai people once more and finally expel the Burmese from Thai soil. He established a new capital at Thonburi, on the opposite bank of the Chao Phya river from Bangkok, and was proclaimed King Taksin, the title being a combination of his given name and his

149

former rank. He ruled the country until the establishment of the Rattanakosin period in 1782 when Bangkok was made Thailand's capital.

Taksin is thus a special hero to the people of Tak and is commemorated by a statue at the northern end of town 600m on the right down the side road (H 12) off H 1. The lifesize seated statue of Taksin is housed in an orange-roofed pavilion the walls of which are decorated with murals depicting scenes from his life.

On the opposite side of the road from the Taksin pavilion is Tak's only other major monument, **Wat Bot Mani Sibunruang**. Most noteworthy here is the **chedi** with a gilded top and the old **viharn** built in typical northern style. A modern **bot** houses the Buddha image of **Luang Phor Buddhamon**, an excellent example of the Sukhothai style.

Apart from these two landmarks, Tak possesses a few interesting wooden houses, a pond and public gardens at the southern end and, of course, the river which, since Tak faces west, is especially attractive at sunset. Yet despite the relative lack of attractions, Tak, with one good first class hotel, the Viang Tak, makes a perfect base for day trips. To the east is Sukhothai (see P.132); to the southeast are the ruins of Kamphaeng Phet and to the west is Mae Sot and the Burmese border. All three destinations are within 70-80km of Tak.

Excursion to Mae Sot. The road to Mae Sot and the Burmese border (H 105) turns off right from H 1 3.1km past the bridge over the Ping river just south of Tak.

Lansang National Park. At KM 12.4 a side road leads left off H 105 and goes 1.4km to the entrance to Lansang National Park (admission 20 baht per car), a picturesque spot featuring a series of waterfalls. The first waterfall, 200m beyond the entrance, is minute but 2km further along the narrow track, which parallels a small stream and passes through a bamboo grove, are far more impressive falls.

Here, amid a pretty clearing in the jungle laid out with picnic tables, are Lansang Falls where the stream tumbles steeply over a series of rocky ledges. Wooden steps and bamboo bridges allow for close-up views while 750m and 2.1km farther up respectively are two other waterfalls, **Pha Phung** and **Pha The.**

Doi Musoe. Beyond the turnoff to Lansang H 105 begins to climb and curve as the hills start to close in producing some extremely beautiful scenery. Just before KM 26 a dirt road on the left goes up to Doi Musoe. The track passes a Lisu village after 1.5km and then, almost next door, a Meo settlement. A little farther along is the entrance to one of the Agricultural Department's experimental stations developing the cultivation of coffee and avocado pears.

By the entrance to the agricultural station the track makes a sharp hairpin bend to the left and after 700m comes to a fork. To the left lies the Hilltribe Centre run by the Ministry of the Interior; to the right a very rough track goes 1.1km to the largish Muser village of **Um-Yom**. This sprawling settlement of houses raised up on stilts is somewhat overrun by dogs, pigs, chickens and the small sturdy horses kept by the tribespeople but does give a good insight into authentic hilltribe life.

There are a number of other hilltribe villages in the area, the easiest of which to reach is the Muser settlement of **Sompuey**, 1km left of H 105 3km past the Doi Musoe turnoff. A little farther along the highway is a string of stalls on the right where the tribespeople sell their produce — however, bottles of Mekong whiskey and Singha beer seem more prevalent than the piles of vegetables.

H 105 begins to descend into the Mae Nam Lamao valley 5.7km beyond the hilltribe stalls and eventually crosses the river before climbing once more into the hills. At the top of the pass, near KM 62, a sheer limestone outcrop forms a narrows and at the base of the cliff on the right is a spirit house to **San Jaopoh Pawo**. Here, on passing, drivers will **wai** and ask for a safe journey. Another spirit house, also on the right, to **Khun Sam Chon** lies a little farther on. From here H 105 descends into the plain of Mae Sot.

Mae Sot. Four kilometres before the town of Mae Sot the highway comes to a three-way junction: to the left H 1090 heads south and parallels the Burmese border; straight on leads into the town centre; to the right H 1085 goes north to Mae Ramard. The right-hand fork also serves as a by-pass to Mae Sot's busy and congested centre and one can loop around the town before continuing straight on 6.7km to the Moei river which forms the border with Burma.

Mae Sot is a busy seemingly prosperous little frontier town and has a charm all its own created by the pleasant mix of Burmese and Thai influences.

A trip to the border just beyond is interesting insofar as one can watch a lively trade as goods are ferried back and forth across the river. A few shops along the banks sells Burmese products including rubies and sapphires for which that country is noted but the quality of the stones here is not high.

As land entry into Burma is forbidden to non-Thais, the traveller must retrace steps back along H 105 to Tak.

Excursion to Kamphaeng Phet. The historic town of Kamphaeng Phet, dating from the Sukhothai period, is situated 67km southeast of Tak off to the left of H 1. To enter the town turn left at KM 354 on to H 101. Kamphaeng Phet proper lies 4.4km away across the bridge over the Ping river but immediately after turning onto H 101 the massive red/brown laterite bricks of the ruined **Phom Toong Setti** fort can be seen on the right. A little farther on, also on the right, are the ruins of four or five **chedis**, one of which, quite close to the road, is in a good state of preservation and is a typical example of the Sukhothai style. Then, on the left just before the bridge, a path leads to **Wat Boromathat** where three ruined **chedis** of the old temple remain although the high **chedi** dates from the Rattanakosin period.

This area on the west bank of the Ping river is the site of the former city of **Chakangrao** which predates Kamphaeng Phet, the latter being constructed when the Sukhothai kings decided for strategic reasons that a settlement would be better located on the east bank.

Kamphaeng Phet (the name literally means 'diamond wall') was the third major centre of the Sukhothai kingdom which united the Thai people in the 13th century. The town, however, achieved its importance later than Sukhothai itself and the second satellite of Si Satchanalai, and as such its ruins display in the main a post classical Sukhothai style.

Much of old Kamphaeng Phet was rebuilt by the Sukhothai King Li Thai (1347 — c 1368) who was a devout patron of the Sri Lankan school of Buddhism, the influences of which can be seen in the architectural styles of many of the town's former temples and monasteries.

The other notable point about the history of Kamphaeng Phet is that it was here that the Sukhothai kingdom finally submitted to the more powerful kingdom of Ayutthaya that had swiftly established itself farther south. In 1378, King Boromaraja I of Ayutthaya laid seige to Kamphaeng Phet after earlier, unsuccessful attempts to take Sukhothai and was eventually rewarded by the old kingdom's submission to become a vassal state of Ayutthaya.

To reach the ruins of old Kamphaeng Phet continue straight on past the roundabout that lies across the bridge (to the right leads into the new town where the hotels are; to the left H 101 skirts around to continue its

Khong Larn, near
Kamphaeng Phet

way northeast to Sukhothai) and then turn left at the junction in front of the town hall.

A few metres past the town hall on the right is the **museum** (open Wednesday to Sunday 8.30 a.m. to 12 noon and 1.00 p.m. to 4.00 p.m.; admission is free except for 2 baht on Saturday and Sunday). This is a good starting point as it gives a fine introduction to the art and former magnificence of old Kamphaeng Phet. The museum contains a selection of bronzes, stucco work and ceramics with its prime exhibit being a 16th century lifesize bronze statue of Siva, one of the finest examples of its kind in Thailand. It is on the first floor that you will find the examples of Sukhothai art while the ground floor contains exhibits from Lopburi, Chiang Saen, Ayutthaya and Rattanakosin periods.

Across the road from the museum is the first of the major ruins to be encountered, **Wat Phra That**, which comprises a main **chedi** surrounded by columns and two smaller **chedis**.

Directly next to Wat Phra That are the more impressive remains of **Wat Phra Keo**. Here low walls survive to give a good idea of the original ground plan of the temple and the laterite platform is surmounted by a highly disfigured image. Behind is the **chedi** flanked by two other badly weathered figures. A little beyond, however, remain two extremely fine seated Buddhas the faces of which masterfully display a sense of serenity. In front of these two statues is a reclining Buddha.

A few metres farther on the right is the pool of **Sra Mon** while on the left by the junction with H 101 is a colorful and highly decorated shrine enclosing the **Lak Muang** (city pillar). Next to this is a large plan giving a clear indication of the location of the major monuments.

From the Lak Muang turn left onto H 101 and after 200m turn right on to a narrow lane that passes the ruins of the **Chao Chan** sentry post. From a right turn after another 300m, the road leads past the old city walls and dried-up moat to the ruins of, first, **Phom Chao Indra** fort and, 700m beyond, those of **Phom Phet** fort. These were, respectively, the southern and northern corners of the fortifications and the massive laterite bricks are quite well preserved (indicating the strength of the 'diamond' walls).

By retracing one's steps back to H 101 and continuing on for 300m past the Lak Muang one comes to a laterite track on the left that leads to the several ruined monuments that lie outside the city walls.

The most important of these are **Wat Phra Non**, the temple of the reclining Buddha, **Wat Phra Si Iriyaboth** and **Wat Chang Rob**. Dominating the former is the main **bot** which dates probably from the Ayutthaya period but the ruins of the older sanctuary containing the reclining Buddha can still be seen.

Wat Phra Si Iriyaboth is distinguished by its **mondop** which has niches containing large statues representing the four main Buddha postures and hence its name — **si** is 'four' and **iriyaboth** means 'postures.' Today, only the standing posture is in reasonably good condition while the walking, seated and reclining statues have largely fallen into decay.

Wat Chang Rob, the temple of the elephants, is remarkable for its massive **chedi** of which only the base and lower levels survive. The base was originally surrounded by rows of laterite and stucco elephants (a Sri Lankan influence) but only the row of support statues on one side are still in good condition and virtually complete. Nevertheless, a good deal of the other stucco decoration around the base can be seen even if only in outline in places.

Proceeding northeast several other minor monuments lie off to the left of H 101, the last of which are **Wat Chao Awat Yai** and **Wat Chao Awat Noi**, the latter being the one ruin that is on the right-hand side of the road. From here H 101 carries on for 77km to reach Sukhothai.

Khong Larn Waterfall. The ruins of the ancient town of Kamphaeng Phet are undoubtedly the most important attraction in the area although a side trip to Khong Larn waterfall can also be recommended.

To reach Khong Larn return to H 1 and continue south for 8.2km before turning right just past KM 346 on to H 1117 which goes 36.6km to the village of Khong Larn. At the village turn right on to a dirt track and after 4.9km take the left-hand fork. After 3km a path leads straight on to a Yao hilltribe village while the turning to the left crosses a bridge over a small stream and reaches the waterfall after a steep and extremely rutted 2.5km stretch.

Isolated in the midst of virgin forest, Khong Larn waterfall is an impressive sight with the water tumbling down a broad, steep 90m high rocky slope. It would be at its most spectacular during the rainy season but, unfortunately, at that time the track would be impassable to all but the most robust vehicles.

Return from Tak to Chiang Mai

An alternative routing to Highways 1 and 11 back to Chiang Mai is H 106, the Old Chiang Mai Road as it is known, since this was the main access to the city before the opening of the Superhighway from Lampang. It is a slower but more attractive route.

H 106 swings northwest off H 1 at Thoen and the first 12km are easy going but after that the road begins to pass over the mountains and for the next 16km it snakes its way along with the mountain on the left and stunning vistas off to the right. It is a spectacular although painfully slow journey and the road is narrow but fortunately it is rarely used these days and there is little on-coming traffic to contend with.

After KM 28 the road descends into a fertile valley and from mountain scenery the surroundings suddenly change to a pleasant setting of paddy fields, banana plantations and the occasional sleepy hamlet.

Major turnoffs encountered along the way are: Mae Ping National Park 46km off to the left just before KM 47; a laterite road on the left by KM 74 going the 33km to Doi Tao at the northern end of Mae Ping Lake, and just beyond KM 118 a side road goes left to near Chom Thong 23km away.

Apart from the initial mountain scenery, the first major attraction along H 106 is **Wat Phra Bard Takpha**, standing on a hill 1km off to the right by KM 136. Legend has it that Lord Buddha once came to this site and requested a disciple to lay out his robe on a rock to dry. Afterwards the rock is supposed to have taken on the shape of the folds of the robe and there is indeed a kind of corrugated one behind the main **viharn** — though if this were where the robe was laid out it must have been many metres wide.

The several buildings in the compound are modern and extremely colourful and ornate. In front of the door on the left side of the **viharn** is a small shrine covering a child-size footprint that is believed to be holy. Inside in the centre is a deep depression where there are two giant Buddha footprints partially covered in gold leaf. Directly above this well is a shrine containing four seated bronze Buddhas facing each of the cardinal points.

The **viharn** was built by the famous monk Sri Vichai in 1930 but it is believed that a temple existed on the site since the reign of Queen Chama Devi of Haripunchai (Lamphun).

Behind the **viharn** is a small **bot** and a shallow cave containing two statues of monks. Behind are the buildings of the monks' quarters in a separate compound.

Modern though the temple is it nevertheless possesses a quiet charm and the tranquil location is enhanced by a fine view over the surrounding plain and hills beyond.

Back on H 106 the old **chedi** of **Wat Phra Than** is on the left 3.5km beyond the turnoff to Wat Phra Bard Takpha, and 2.1km farther on, just after KM 141, are two old Burmese-style **chedis** flanking each side of the road — the spot is also marked by a giant tree on the right.

A little beyond KM 143, H 106 enters the town of Pa Sang and then continues on to Lamphun from where it is 26km to Chiang Mai.

TRAVEL INFORMATION ON THE NORTH

HOTELS IN THE NORTH

Note: hotels are listed alphabetically and category is indicated by room rate. Prices of suites not included. Rates subject to change.

Bhumipol Dam

Guesthouse 100, Bhumipol Dam. 26 rooms, air-conditioned, 210-280 baht. Bangkok reservations: 424-3805.

Chiang Mai

A&P, 41 Moon Muang Road. Tel: 236309. 42 rooms, partly air-conditioned, 150-250 baht.
Anodard, 57-9 Rajamanka Road. Tel: 235353, 235755. 150 rooms, partly air-conditioned, 250-400 baht.
Bangkok, 15/2 Moo 3 Suthep Road. Tel: 221746. 9 rooms, partly air-conditioned, 100-200 baht.
Bua Luang Bungalow, 16/1 Huay Kaeo Road. Tel: 221678. 24 Bungalows, air-conditioned, 300 baht.
Chang Puak, 133 Chotana Road. Tel: 221755-6. 57 rooms, partly air-conditioned, 190-400 baht.
Chaw Phet, 53/4 Sitthiwong Road. Tel: 234119. 34 rooms, partly air-conditioned, 80-150 baht.
Chiang Inn, 100 Chang Klan Road. Tel: 235655, 236220. 170 rooms, air-conditioned, 962-1,114 baht. Bangkok reservations: 251-6883, 251-7729.
Chiang Mai President, 226 Vichayanon Road. Tel: 235116. 140 rooms, air-conditioned, 886 baht. Bangkok reservations: 392-5530-6.
Diamond, 33/10 haroenpratet Road. Tel: 234155. 145 rooms, partly air-conditioned, 280-583 baht.
Chiang Mai Hills, 18 Huay Kaeo Road. Tel: 221254-5. 82 rooms, air-conditioned, 633-759 baht. Bangkok reservations: 235-0240-5, 2332861.
Chiang Mai Palace, 112, Chang Klan Road. Tel: 236835, 236962. 198 rooms, air-conditioned, 805 baht. Bangkok reservations: 234-8971-5, 2332305-6.

Orchid Chiang Mai, 100-102 Huay Kaeo Road. Tel: 221625. 267 rooms, air-conditioned, 1,012-1,898 baht. Bangkok reservations: 235-4167-8.

Kochasarn, 53 Kochasarn Road. Tel: 236063. 27 rooms, partly air-conditioned, 90-200 baht.

Lanna, 137 Chotana Road. Tel: 221733. 26 rooms, air-conditioned, 465 baht.

Miami, 11 Chaisripoom Road. Tel: 235240. 17 rooms, 100-120 baht.

Mittraparp, 94-98 Rajawong Road. Tel: 235436. 118 rooms, partly air-conditioned, 110-200 baht.

Montha, 20 Loy Kroa Soi 3 Road. Tel: 235937. 23 rooms, partly air-conditioned, 120-200 baht.

Montri, 2-6 Raddamnoen Road. Tel: 236910, 236970. 92 rooms, partly air-conditioned, 150-290 baht.

Morakot, 39 Chotana Soi 4 Road. Tel: 222618. 18 rooms, partly air-conditioned, 80-180 baht.

Muang Mai, 502 Huay Kaeo Road. Tel: 221392, 221418. 155 rooms, air-conditioned, 532-658 baht.

Muang Thong, 5 Rajmanka Road. Tel: 236438. 21 rooms, 70-100 baht.

Nakornmai Lodge, 4/2 Chiang Mai-San Kamphaeng Road. Tel: 235352, 235961. 105 rooms, partly air-conditioned, 80-120 baht.

Nakornping, 43 Rajawong Road. Tel: 236024. 22 rooms, 80-100 baht.

New Asia, 55 Rajawong Road. Tel 235288. 204 rooms, partly air-conditioned, 200-400 baht.

New Chiang Mai, 22 Chaiyapoom Road. Tel: 236561, 236766. 45 rooms, partly air-conditioned, 130-220 baht.

Patchara, 404/8 Moo 5 Santitham Road. Tel: 221335. 80 rooms, air-conditioned, 300 baht. Bangkok reservations: 391-3287, 391-7808.

Porn Ping, 46-48 Charoenpratet Road. Tel: 235643. 180 rooms, air-conditioned, 480-759 baht. Bangkok reservations: 251-7392, 251-3689.

Poy Luang, 146 Superhighway. Tel: 234633, 234923. 225 rooms, air-conditioned, 886-1,012 baht. Bangkok reservations: 391-0320, 391-0100.

Prince, 3 Taiwang Road. Tel: 236396, 236744. 112 rooms, partly air-conditioned, 220-400 baht.

Railway Hotel, 471 Charoenmuang Road. Tel: 236755, 236983. 76 rooms, air-conditioned, 264-363 baht. Bangkok reservations: 233-7061, 233-0341 ext. 223.
Rincome, 301 Huay Kaeo Road. Tel: 221044, 221123. 160 rooms, air-conditioned, 845-1,100 baht. Bangkok reservations: 252-6118, 252-6087.
Rintr Hotel, 99/9 Huay Kaeo Road. Tel: 221483. 33 rooms, air-conditioned, 600-759 baht.
Rom Poh, Ta Pae Road. 20 rooms, 20-30 baht.
Roongruang, 398 Ta Pae Road. Tel: 236746. 16 rooms, 80-100 baht.
Sangtawee, 7/2 Huay Kaeo Road, Soi Wat Chang Kien. Tel: 221099. 50 rooms, partly air-conditioned, 120-360 baht.
Setthakit, 47 near Railway Station. Tel: 236765, 235589. 80 rooms, partly air-conditioned, 120-280 baht.
Sri Prakad, 35 Chiang Mai-Lamphun Road. Tel: 236272. 64 rooms, 60-70 baht.
Sri Rajawong, 103 Rajawong Road. Tel: 235864. 20 rooms, 60-80 baht.
Sri Santitham, 15 Santitham Road. Tel: 221585. 26 rooms, partly air-conditioned, 70-150 baht.
Sri Tokyo, 63 Chang Klan Road. Tel: 235622. 144 rooms, partly air-conditioned, 210-490 baht.
Suan Buak Hadd, Samlarn Road. Tel: 221406. 14 rooms, 100-120 baht.
Sumit, 198 Rajapakinai Road. Tel: 235996, 236014. 99 rooms, partly air-conditioned, 140-290 baht. Bangkok resrvations: 279-4525-6.
Suriwongse, 110 Chang Klan Road. Tel: 236789, 236733. 168 rooms, air-conditioned, 886-1,012 baht. Bangkok reservations: 251-2066.
Thai Charoen, 164-166 Ta Pae Road. Tel: 236640. 32 rooms, 60-100 baht.
Wieng Kaew, 7/9 Huay Kaeo Road. Tel: 221549. 55 rooms, partly air-conditioned, 160-290 baht.
Y.M.C.A., 2/4 Mengrai-Rasmee Road, Tel: 221819, 221821. 33 rooms, partly air-conditioned, 85-255 baht.

Guesthouses (average rates approximately 50-100 baht)
Chumpol, 89 Charoenpratet Road. Tel: 234526. 24 rooms.

Chiang Mai International, 302 Manee Noprarat Road.
Tel: 221180. 16 rooms.
Chiang Mai, 91 Charoenpratet Road. Tel: 236501.
28 rooms.
Galare, 7-7/1 Charoenpratet Road. Tel: 233885.
16 rooms.
Gemini, 22 Rajdamnern Road. Tel: 236451. 15 rooms.
Happy House, 11/1 Changmoi Kao Road. Tel: 234969.
Lek House, 22 Chaiyapoom Road. 12 rooms.

Chiang Rai

Krung Thong, 412 Sanumbean Road. Tel: 311033,
311212. 100 rooms, partly air-conditioned, 110-220 baht.
Rama, 331/4 Trirat Road. Tel: 311344. 44 rooms, partly
air-conditioned, 150-400 baht.
Reong Nakorn, 25 Reong Nakorn Road. Tel: 311566,
311567. 61 rooms, partly air-conditioned, 120-260
baht.
Suknirand, 424/1 Banphaprakarn Road. Tel: 311055.
105 rooms, partly air-conditioned 120-240 baht.
Wiang Inn, 893 Phaholyotin Road. Tel: 311543,
311533. 160 rooms, air-conditioned, 370-560 baht.

Chiang Saen

Chiang Saen Guesthouse, 45 Mekong Riverside.
10 rooms, 30-60 baht.
Poon Suk. 5 rooms, 40-60 baht.

Fang

Aung Kam. 10 bungalows, 80-120 baht.
Metta. 11 rooms, 30-50 baht.
Sri Chukij. 30 rooms, 30-120 baht.
Wiang Fang. 23 rooms, 30-90 baht.
Wiang Kaew. 8 bungalows, 80-120 baht.
Y.M.C.A. Dormitory with 12 beds, 20 baht.

Kamphaeng Phet

Chakangraw, Thesa Road. Tel: 711315, 711325-6.
116 rooms, air-conditioned, 200-400 baht.
Nawarat, Thesa Road. Tel: 711211, 711106, 711219.
80 rooms, air-conditioned, 200-250 baht.

Phet Hotel, 99 Vichit Road, Soi 3. Tel: 711283-5.
229 rooms, air-conditioned, 340-390 baht. Bangkok
reservations: 251-6512, 251-6932, 251-6340.

Lampang

Asia Lampang, 229 Bunyawas. Tel: 217844, 217761.
64 rooms, 120-314 baht.
Khelangnakorn, 720 Suandok Road. Tel: 217137.
19 rooms, 30-50 baht.
Lampang, 696 Suandok Road. Tel: 217311, 217312.
52 rooms, 70-160 baht.
Rom Sri, 142 Bunyawas. Tel: 217054. 40 rooms, 60-150
baht.
Siam Hotel, 260/26-29 Chatchai Road. Tel: 217472,
217277, 217642. 84 rooms, 100-200 baht.
Suandok, 168 Bunyawas. Tel: 217721, 217586.
35 rooms, 100-160 baht.
Tipchang Garnet Lampang, 54/22 Tarkra Noi, Soptui.
Tel: 218078, 218337, 218450, 218864, 218822.
125 rooms, air-conditioned, 400-500 baht.

Mae Hong Son

Mae Tee, 55 Khunlumprapas Road. Tel: 611141.
29 rooms, partly air-conditioned, 100-220 baht.
Mitrniyom, 90 Khunlumprapas Road. Tel: 611139.
38 rooms, partly air-conditioned, 100-220 baht.

Mae Sa Valley

Mae Sa Valley Resort, c/o North West Tour,
Suriwongse Hotel, Chiang Mai. Tel: 236789, 236733.
30 rooms, 517-572 baht.
Suan Rintr, near Mae Sa Waterfall, c/o Rintr Hotel,
Chiang Mai. Tel: 221483. 15 units, 480-540 baht.

Mae Sai

Mae Sai Hotel, 125/5 Phaholyothin Road. 25 rooms,
100-150 baht.
Top North, 521/7-8 Phaholyothin Road. 20 rooms,
100-150 baht.
Sinwatana (Siwhong), 24 Phaholyothin Road. 22
rooms, 60-100 baht.

Mae Sariang

Mitaree. 50 rooms, partly air-conditioned, 80-280 baht.

Nan

Amorn Sri, 91 Anantavoradej Road. 16 rooms, 50-80 baht.
Dhevaraj, 466 Sumondhevaraj Road. Tel: 710095, 710212. 154 rooms, partly air-conditioned, 150-400 baht.
Sukkasem, 29-31 Anantavoradej Road. Tel: 710141. 41 rooms, partly air-conditioned, 60-180 baht.

Phitsanulok

Amarintr Nakorn, 3/1 Chaophaya Road. Tel: 258588, 258331. 130 rooms, air-conditioned, 240-370 baht.
Nanchao, 242 Baromtrilokanart Road. Tel: 259511-3. 115 rooms, partly air-conditioned, 140-536 baht.
The Rajapruk, Visutkasat Road. Tel: 258477, 258788, 258789, 259660, 259740. 101 rooms, air-conditioned, 260-360 baht.

Phrae

Nakorn Phrae, Rajadamnern Road. Tel: 511122, 511024. 165 rooms, partly air-conditioned, 140-260 baht.

Sukhothai

Kitmongkol, 43 Singhawat. Tel: 611193. 53 rooms, partly air-conditioned, 70-160 baht.
Pongprasert, 92/6 Nikornkasem. Tel: 611656 29 rooms, partly air-conditioned, 60-180 baht.
Rajthanee, 229 Charodvitheethong Road. Tel: 611031, 611038. 27 rooms, air-conditioned, 210-350 baht.
Sawaddiphong, 56/2-5 Singhawat. Tel: 611567, 611324. 40 rooms, partly air-conditioned, 60-200 baht.
Shinawat, 145-146 Charodvitheethong Road. Tel: 611385, 611689. 41 rooms, partly air-conditioned, 70-180 baht.
Sukhothai, 15/5 Singhawat. Tel: 611133. 50 rooms, partly air-conditioned, 70-180 baht.

Tak

Mae Ping, Mahadthai Bamrung Road. Tel: 511807,
511819. 45 rooms, partly air-conditioned, 40-100 baht.
Sa-Nguan Thai, Taksin Road. Tel: 511265. 42 rooms,
partly air-conditioned, 60-160 baht.
Viang Tak, 25/3 Mahadthai Bamrung Road. Tel:
511910, 511950. 100 rooms, air-conditioned, 390-570
baht. Bangkok reservations: 233-2690, 234-4885.

Uttaradit

Phor Vanich Hotel 1, 174 Samranruen Road. Tel:
411008. 30 rooms, partly air-conditioned, 80-170 baht.
Phor Vanich Hotel 2, 1-5 Sriudtra Road. Tel: 411499,
411749. 73 rooms, partly air-conditioned, 90-200 baht.
Thanothai, 149/53 Kasemraj Road. Tel: 411669.
23 rooms, partly air-conditioned, 90-180 baht.
Vivat Hotel, 159 Borroma-art (outside town on H 102).
Tel: 411778. 80 rooms, partly air-conditioned, 120-400
baht.

FESTIVALS AND HOLIDAYS

No one loves a festival more than the Northern Thai and in addition to those events in the national calendar, many other affairs are celebrated in the North, especially in Chiang Mai. Most are characterised by bright lights, beauty contests, parades, food and lots of noise; visitors are generally welcome to participate. Most dates vary from year to year. The Tourism Authority of Thailand annually issues a pamphlet called 'Thailand Events' which gives exact dates for the year. The events listed below are the major festivals and those which are official holidays are marked. Official holidays also occur on April 6, May 5, October 23 and December 10. Government offices and banks are closed on these days.

JANUARY
Chiang Mai Winter Fair held over the first week of the month at the Municipal Sports Stadium.

FEBRUARY
Makha Bucha on the night of the full moon commemorates Buddha's first sermon to his 1,250 disciples. Just after moonrise, worshippers carrying flowers, lighted candles and incense sticks walk in procession three times around the temple. You are welcome to join them. (Official holiday.)

Chiang Mai Flower Carnival held on the first weekend of the month and marked by parade of colourful flower floats, beauty contests and flower shows.

APRIL
Songkran (April 13-15) is the traditional New Year and is celebrated by everyone throwing water at everyone else. As a tourist you are fair game and normally the likeliest target. Don't take anything with you that cannot stand a soaking. If the latter includes

yourself, stay in your hotel room; it's the only safe place (maybe). Festival also includes procession of important Buddha images and a Miss Songkran beauty contest. (Official holiday only on the 13th outside Chiang Mai).

MAY

Visakha Bucha commemorates the birth, enlightenment and death of Buddha. Like **Makha Bucha**, it occurs on the full moon night and is marked by a triple procession around the temple. In Chiang Mai there is a tradition of walking up to Wat Phrathat on Doi Suthep to pay homage at the Buddha relic and make merit. (Official holiday).

Intakin Festival, Chiang Mai's City Pillar homage ceremony, lasting 7 days and 7 nights, takes place at Wat Chedi Luang and is to invoke blessings of peace, happiness and prosperity for the city and its people.

Lychee Fair at Fang celebrates the lychee harvest with contest for best fruit and lychee beauty queen.

JUNE

City Merit-Making Ceremony at city gates and city centre to mark the anniversary of the founding of Chiang Mai as the northern capital.

JULY

Asahala Bucha commemorates Buddha's first sermon to his first five disciples. It marks the beginning of the three-month **Khao Phansa** (often referred to as Buddhist Lent) during which monks remain in their monasteries to meditate. It occurs on the full moon night and is celebrated by a candlelight circumambulation of the temple (Official holiday.)

AUGUST

August 12 is Her Majesty Queen Sirikit's birthday. The streets are brightly lit in celebration.

Lamyai Fair celebrates lamyai harvest with displays of best fruit and beauty contests. Biggest fair is in Lamphun.

Orchid Fair in Chiang Mai organized to promote and select best varieties of orchids.

OCTOBER

Tod Kathin marks the end of **Khao Phansa**, the rainy season and the harvest and is celebrated by colourful, noisy processions to the temples to present gifts and donations to the monks. It lasts the entire month starting from the end of **Khao Phansa**.

Dhevo-Rohana Offering Ceremony is an annual ceremony organized by Chiang Mai University to encourage the tradition of offering dried foodstuffs to monks on the first day of the waning moon of the 11th lunar month, the day on which Buddha descended from heaven and returned to earth. Celebrated at the temple on the university campus.

NOVEMBER

The **Loy Krathong Festival** is unique to Thailand and is perhaps the most beautiful of all its celebrations. Dating from the Sukhothai kingdom of 700 years ago, it takes place on the night of the full moon (and also on the following night in Chiang Mai and Sukhothai). The high point is the launching of tiny floral boats with candles, incense sticks and snippets of hair into rivers and ponds all over Thailand. It was started one full moon evening when King Ramkamhaeng's beautiful young wife, Nang Noppamat, placed a similar candlelit boat in the water to amuse her husband sitting in a

Loy Krathong Festival, Sukhothai

pavilion downstream. Buy a Krathong and join the others at the riverbank and enjoy a magical night. On the second night of the festival in Chiang Mai there is a parade and contest of large illuminated krathong floats bearing beautiful girls in Thai and northern costumes down the main street to Chiang Mai Municipal landing.

DECEMBER

His Majesty King Bhumipol's birthday on December 5 is marked by brightly lit streets. (Official holiday.)

Bor Sang Umbrella is a two-day event to promote the umbrella making industry at Bor Sang and is marked by elephant parades, displays of umbrellas and a beauty contest.

New Year's Eve is as boisterous in Thailand as it is elsewhere in the world with everyone blowing off steam and readying themselves to enter the new year afresh. (Official holidays on Dec. 31 and Jan. 1.)

HILLTRIBES

Not the least of the North's attractions are the several groups of hilltribe people who inhabit the cool, jungle-covered mountain areas of the region. These are semi-nomadic tribes that over the years have migrated into Thailand from southern China. Each group is ethnically different and has its own language, customs, religion and distinctive dress which, along with a tradition of independence from any form of central government, are proudly preserved.

The seven principal tribes are: Akha (Igo); Lahu (Muser); Lawa; Lisu; Karen; Meo (Hmong) and Yao. Their numbers have been variously estimated at between 250,000 and 500,000 with the Karen and Meo being the most numerous.

The visitor is generally made welcome at any hilltribe village and is free to wander around and to observe scenes of daily life, the colourful costumes, especially of the women and children, and traditional handicrafts such as weaving on primitive hand looms. The presence of the hilltribes is also felt in the number of handicrafts for sale — notably silver jewellery and embroidered dresses, jackets etc — both in towns such as Chiang Mai and at the villages themselves. Note that while the tribespeople live largely independent lives they have not been backward in catching on to the lucrative tourist industry, and even in some remote villages hawkers push their wares with some persistence. Generally, however, the farther away from a town the settlement is, the more authentic and unchanged it is likely to be.

Although adding a touch of colour and exotic charm to the region, the presence of the hilltribes in northern Thailand has not been without its problems. Their traditional and, until recently, only cash crop has been the opium poppy and, moreover, their slash-and-burn farming technique has led to the destruction of forests and watersheds and to soil erosion. At the same time their standard of living is in most cases extremely low.

In the last few years, however, a number of government and Royal projects have been set up to provide social, medical and educational aid to the hilltribes and, more importantly, to give assistance in introducing alternative cash crops to the opium poppy. The latter is aimed at both eradicating a social evil and at raising living standards — contrary to popular belief, it is not the growers of opium that make the big money out of the drug trade and the cultivation of fruit and vegetables, under proper conditions, can earn the hilltribe farmer much more.

Such projects are proving successful and the acreage of land under poppy cultivation is declining while the standard of living among hilltribes is rising. All this does not mean, however, that traditional tribal culture is being eroded. Typical villages with an unchanged way of life still abound and traditional customs, beliefs and handicrafts remain.

Akha

The Akha is one of the smallest tribes in Thailand and rank as probably the poorest and most underdeveloped. These tribespeople migrated from China's Yunnan province to the North via the Shan states of Burma and today the largest concentration of villages is in the Mae Chan and Mae Sai districts north of Chiang Rai.

Akha Hilltribe Headdress

171

Like most tribespeople, the Akha are animists and attach great importance to the souls of the dead. Reverence of spirits is most readily witnessed in the spirit houses that adorn village compounds and the bamboo arch at the entrance to a village which is also raised to the spirits. Male and female fertility symbols are usually placed at the base of these arches.

Akha women dress in short black blouses and skirts, often embroidered and decorated with pieces of dyed cloth. Beads, silver necklaces and plates are common adornments and headdresses are colourful and highly decorated affairs. As with most other tribes, the men now tend to dress in the typical costume of the ordinary Thai farmer.

Karen

The most ubiquitous of the hilltribes, the Karen, are of Tibeto-Burman stock and are indigenous to southeastern Burma although many migrated early into Thailand, some even before the Thais themselves. Their villages can be found throughout most of the North, except in the far eastern part of the region, but they are most noticeable along the journey from Chiang Mai to Mae Sariang and Mae Hong Son.

The costume of the women is usually a long, loose one-piece dress. Only married women sport colours and the single girl is decked out in plain white.

Lahu

The Lahu are of Tibetan stock and come originally from southern China. They are scattered in small numbers throughout the North and tend to be more nomadic and more easy-going than other tribes and consequently they are the least known. There are four principal groupings although all refer to themselves as Lahu while the Thai name is Muser. Traditional dress for the women is a long narrow skirt and a jacket generally worn open. Broad strips of coloured cloth decorate collar, breast, sleeves and hem.

Lawa

Unlike the other hilltribes, the Lawa are most likely indigenous to northern Thailand being of Mon-Khmer stock. They inhabited the region long before the establishment of the Lannathai kingdom. Today they are most common south and west of Chiang Mai around Hot, Mae Sariang and Mae Hong Son. One of the largest Lawa settlements is Bor Luang which lies on the road from Hot to Mae Sariang. This tribe is more settled than most with consolidated villages and households being important elements in the society.

The women generally wear rather plain, smock-like dresses, dark blue for those who are married and white for single girls. If their costume is comparatively undistinguished, the women, nevertheless, are noticeable for their fondness for pipe smoking and are rarely seen without a curved pipe, often adorned with silver, hanging from their mouths.

Lisu

The Lisu are well known for their cultivation of the opium poppy but they are also the most gay-looking and colourful of the northern tribes. The women wear a multi-coloured, long-sleeved blouse reaching to the knees with a waist band and worn over trousers. Their heads are adorned with broad turbans of black cloth decorated with long tassles. The men are not to be outdone in dress and wear long-sleeved black jackets decorated with silver on the shoulders, and either

Lisu Tribespeople

bright green or blue baggy pantaloons. They also often sport a single earring.

Migrating from Tibet via Yunnan and the Shan states, the Lisu are today mostly found in the mountain areas around Chiang Dao, Fang, Mae Hong Son and Tak.

Meo

The Meo, or Hmong, are the most commonly seen tribespeople being less shy than others of venturing into Chiang Mai and other towns to trade in silver jewellery and embroidery work. Some have even become shopkeepers or settled traders.

More Chinese looking in their facial characteristics, the Meo have settled mostly in Chiang Mai, Chiang Rai, Phrae, Lampang and Mae Hong Son provinces. Like the Lisu, they are commonly engaged in the cultivation of opium. They also have a fondness for making and wearing large, chunky items of silver jewellery, frequently worn as symbols of wealth. Apart from a preponderance of silver necklaces, neck rings etc, the women wear jackets and pleated skirts over trousers decorated with fine coloured embroidery.

Yao

Originating from parts of central China, the Yao migrated to Thailand via Burma and Laos mostly between 1910 and 1950. They have a close past relationship with the Chinese and have adopted many Chinese traditions. Accordingly they are generally deemed culturally superior to other tribes. They are concentrated in the northern part of Chiang Mai province, Chiang Rai and Mae Hong Son.

Their dress is quite magnificent with Yao women wearing black blouses and trousers colourfully decorated with intricately designed embroidery and lengths of coloured cloth hanging from the waist. Most distinctive is the bright red or pink 'puff,' rather like a feather boa, worn around the neck of the blouse. Large black or dark blue turbans, often embroidered, are also worn. Silver ornaments and coins are added to the dress during festivals and other important occasions.

THE THAI ELEPHANT

For centuries the elephant has been revered by Thais for its intelligence, strength and usefulness, and it is widely regarded as a symbol of good fortune. The pachyderm has been depicted in countless temple decorations from magnificent carvings to mural paintings. It was once engraved on the coins of old Siam and, from 1819 to 1917, was featured on the national flag — it can still be seen on the ensign of the Royal Thai Navy.

Moreover, hundreds of superstitions and sayings about elephants remain in popular usage with, for example, it being widely believed that to walk beneath an elephant's belly brings good luck. And, of course, any albino or 'white' elephant is deemed the property of the King and the possession of one or more is considered to presage well for the monarch's reign.

Such high esteem is not surprising when it is considered that elephants have historically figured large in the socio-economic development of Thailand. Like a distinctive pattern running through the country's social fabric, they have made their contribution on the battlefield, in royal ceremonies, as symbols of wealth and power and, most significantly of all, as work animals of enormous value and skill.

All this is true for the entire country but it is the North that is the true 'home' of the Thai elephant and where its historical and present day roles can be best appreciated. On the historical side, the **chedi** near the village of Ban Tak commemorates the first recorded battle on elephant back. The superstitious belief in the instinctive powers of elephants is witnessed in King Mengrai's selection of the site for Chiang Rai and in the choosing of locations for **chedis**, notably the placing of relics at Wat Phrathat on Doi Suthep. Then there is the founding of the town of Mae Hong Son which sprung directly from a need to capture and train wild elephants.

Yet it is as a work animal in the teak forests of the North that the elephant has made its greatest contribution. In the task of extracting the highly prized wood from the remote and dense forests and transporting the logs to collection points, the pachyderm has worked less as a beast of burden and more as a partner with man in a pursuit that was formerly one of Thailand's largest foreign exchange earners.

Sadly, today both the teak reserves and the number of elephants are dwindling and gone are the great days when the big teak concessionaires, such as the Borneo Company, Louis T. Leonowens Ltd and the East Asiatic Company, employed hundreds of elephants in the exploitation of the riches of the North. Nevertheless, the diesel engine has not yet totally replaced the pachyderm and the animals are still used by the Government Forest Industry Organization.

When travelling upcountry it is possible to catch a glimpse of an elephant or two at work (except during the hot season when they are rested), but the visitors' best opportunity for seeing these animals at close range is at the several training camps that are scattered around the North. These are mentioned in the foregoing text and the best known establishment is

A Working Elephant

176

the government-run Young Elephant Training Centre near Lampang. All these camps put on early morning shows where the visitor can see how the animals are trained and what tasks — pulling, dragging, lifting, stacking logs either singly or in pairs — they are capable of performing.

Every working elephant has its own **mahout** or handler who will stay with it generally throughout its working life. It is the **mahout's** responsibility not only to direct the animal in its work in the forests but also to feed and take care of it. Although elephants possess incredible strength, they are not as robust as their body weight would suggest and they are prone to illness so constant care is required. Moreover, like man they can suffer from over-work and heat exhaustion and accordingly they work mornings only and have regular holidays. Again like man their best working days are from the age of 16 to 38 and they are generally retired at around 60.

Training begins when the elephant is 3-5 years old and schooling will last for 5-6 years. One of the most tricky tasks is separating the baby elephant from its possessive mother and in especially difficult cases a shaman may be brought in to perform a special ceremony to help bring about the desired effect.

The first lessons are designed to get the elephant acquainted with its **mahout** and to familiarise it with the basic words of command. Subsequently, after being put through the morning ritual of a bath in the river — fun for the elephant but also necessary for its well being — the pupils are taken through walking exercises, alone, in pairs and in procession, taught how to assist the **mahout** to mount and dismount and how to pick up small objects. Advanced schooling teaches the elephant the various methods of manoeuvering timber in forest conditions and finally it is made familiar with the noise of the logging machines.

The lengthy period of training is expensive but the elephant, once a mature worker, more than pays back the investment. Should you for some strange reason want to buy a fully trained elephant, a good one would put you back by at least 100,000 baht.

THAI CUSTOMS

Thais are remarkably tolerant of foreign idiosyncrasies, a trait which has endeared them to many visitors. There are, however, a few cultural no-nos that the foreigner should be aware of. Most of the taboos have to do with the feet. This is a remnant from Brahmanic belief which says that the head is the crown of the body, the centre of intelligence and its cleanest part. This is why a masseuse bathing a customer will instantly beg his forgiveness if she accidently touches his face or hair (no apologies for other parts of the anatomy).

The rest of the body is progressively dirtier as one travels down to the feet. Thus it is considered impolite to point the feet at anyone, kick a person or step over a reclining body. It is also improper to touch anyone but small children on the head. For women there is a special taboo: they cannot touch or even brush against a monk for fear of compromising his vow of celibacy. This applies to all women, even the monk's mother.

Tipping is done in the large hotels and restaurants but not in small food shops. Ten per cent is the normal amount. Taxi drivers are not tipped.

If involved in a dispute, keep calm (**jai yen** 'cool heart' the Thais call it, a character trait more important than anything except honouring one's mother and sticking with one's friends in times of trouble), don't shout and, above all, don't fight. The law in Thailand is flexible, judging an incident on its merits rather than according to a hide-bound statute. As elsewhere in the world, it tends to favour the national over the visitor. Violence can only land one in deeper trouble.

Travellers should be aware that there are restrictions regarding the export of Buddha images from Thailand. Buddha images without export permits will be confiscated by customs officials. Yes, even new images!

INDEX